PRAISE FOR *LOST & FOUND*

“Dealing with challenging behaviors? The first goal is to alter your lenses, to understand that challenging behavior is the result of lagging skills. The second is to start solving problems together and teach those skills. *Lost and Found* is a must read.”

—MICHELLE GARCIA WINNER, MA-CCC, SPEECH LANGUAGE PATHOLOGIST; FOUNDER, SOCIAL THINKING

“*Lost and Found* gives ceaders lots of examples for how Dr. Ross Greene's Collaborative & Proactive Solutions (CPS) process works—and how to avoid pitfalls—at every step of the way. The process he describes is the best way to engage kids and adults in mutual problem solving that, at its core, removes blame and replaces it with respect.”

—PEG DAWSON, EDD, NCSP, CO-AUTHOR, *SMART BUT SCATTERED* AND *SMART BUT SCATTERED TEENS*

“For those perplexed by how to positively support students with challenging behavior, *Lost and Found* is a game changer. Greene brings a fresh perspective on the subject and clearly articulates the essentials to get everyone on the upswing,”

—LEAH KUYPERS, MA, OCCUPATIONAL THERAPIST; AUTHOR, *THE ZONES OF REGULATION: A CURRICULUM DESIGNED TO FOSTER SELF-REGULATION AND EMOTIONAL CONTROL*

“Greene's CPS model encourages school staff to look at behaviorally challenging students from a new frame of reference: kids are very capable of providing information about why they're having difficulty mecting certain expectations; they're cager to partner with adults in solving the problems that are affecting their lives; and they're capable of developing new skills. *Lost and Found* provides the tools to help schools abandon old, toxic ways of responding to challenging behavior.”

—DEBRA THIBODEAU,MED, CAS, SCHOOL COUNSELOR, GEORGETOWN, ME

“Throughout *Lost and Found*, the voices of educators are a testament to how this simple, research-based process, done with rigor, results in changing beliefs, practices, and school cultures. Ross Greene should be considered a living, international treasure.”

—PEGGY BLAIR, SUPERINTENDENT OF EDUCATION, AVON MAITLAND DISTRICT SCHOOL BOARD, ONTARIO, CANADA

Lost & Found

Unlocking Collaboration and Compassion to Help Our Most Vulnerable, Misunderstood Students (and All the Rest)

ROSS W. GREENE, PhD

SECOND EDITION

JOSSEY-BASS™
A Wiley Brand

Jossey-Bass
A Wiley Imprint
111 River St, Hoboken, NJ 07030
www.josseybass.com

Jossey-Bass books and products are available through most bookstores. To contact Jossey-Bass directly, call our Customer Care Department within the U.S. at 800–956–7739, outside the U.S. at +1 317 572 3986, or fax +1 317 572 4002.

Wiley also publishes its books in a variety of electronic formats and by print-on-demand. Some material included with standard print versions of this book may not be included in e-books or in print-on-demand. If this book refers to media such as a CD or DVD that is not included in the version you purchased, you may download this material at http://booksupport.wiley.com. For more information about Wiley products, visit www.wiley.com.

Library of Congress Cataloging-in-Publication Data

Names: Greene, Ross W., author. | Jossey-Bass Inc., publisher.
Title: Lost & found : unlocking collaboration and compassion to help our most vulnerable, misunderstood students (and all the rest) / Ross W. Greene, PhD.
Description: Second edition. | [San Francisco] : Jossey-Bass, [2021] | Includes index.
Identifiers: LCCN 2021017296 (print) | LCCN 2021017297 (ebook) | ISBN 9781119813576 (hardback) | ISBN 9781119813590 (adobe pdf) | ISBN 9781119813583 (epub)
Subjects: LCSH: Problem children—Education. | Behavior disorders in children. | Behavior modification.
Classification: LCC LC4801 .G724 2022 (print) | LCC LC4801 (ebook) | DDC 371.93—dc23
LC record available at https://lccn.loc.gov/2021017296
LC ebook record available at https://lccn.loc.gov/2021017297

Cover Design: Paul McCarthy
Cover Art: © Istockphoto | Slobo

SECOND EDITION

SKY10048657_060223

PREVIOUS BOOKS BY ROSS W. GREENE, PHD

The Explosive Child (1998)

Treating Explosive Kids (2005)

Lost at School (2008)

Raising Human Beings (2016)

CONTENTS

Dedicated to my mom, Cynthia Greene,
who taught me a thing or two about empathy,
compassion, and resilience

ABOUT THE AUTHOR

Ross W. Greene, PhD, is the originator of the innovative, evidence-based approach known as Collaborative & Proactive Solutions (CPS), as described in this book and his prior books *The Explosive Child*, *Lost at School*, and *Raising Human Beings*. Dr. Greene served on the faculty at Harvard Medical School for over twenty years, and is currently adjunct professor in the Department of Psychology at Virginia Tech and adjunct professor in the Faculty of Science at University of Technology Sydney in Australia. He is also the founding director of the nonprofit Lives in the Balance (www.livesinthebalance.org), which provides a vast array of free, web-based resources on his model, and advocates on behalf of kids with concerning behaviors and their parents, teachers, and other caregivers. He also developed and executive produced the award-winning documentary film, *The Kids We Lose*. Dr. Greene is the author of numerous articles, chapters, and scientific papers on the effectiveness of the CPS model; the classification of and outcomes in youth with social, emotional, and behavioral challenges; and student-teacher compatibility. He consults to families, schools, inpatient psychiatry units, and residential and juvenile detention facilities throughout the world and lives in Freeport, Maine.

ACKNOWLEDGMENTS

There are many theories and models that influenced the approach to helping kids with concerning behaviors—called *Collaborative & Proactive Solutions* (CPS)—described in this book, including social learning theory, family systems theory, transactional/reciprocal models of development, goodness-of-fit theory, personal construct theory, neuropsychology, and developmental psychopathology. I am indebted to the countless people who exposed me to and taught me about those theories and models, including Dr. Elizabeth Altmaier (then at the University of Florida); Drs. Tom Ollendick and George Clum (at the Department of Psychology at Virginia Tech); and Dr. Mary Ann McCabe and Lorraine Lougee, then at Children's National Medical Center in Washington, DC. Of course, my children—Talia and Jacob (now twenty-three and twenty years old)—have taught me plenty. And the influence of my original teachers—my father, Irving (who is no longer with us), and my mother, Cynthia, to whom this book is dedicated—is inestimable.

But I am especially indebted to the thousands of general and special education classroom teachers, school administrators, paraprofessionals, ed techs, school mental health professionals, and specialists I've had the good fortune to work with and learn from over the past twenty-five years. Despite working under very difficult circumstances, often thanklessly, you've taught me what a huge difference an educator can make in a child's life, most especially those with social, emotional, and behavioral challenges who badly need someone to listen to them, nurture them, and help and care about them. You have my everlasting admiration.

INTRODUCTION

Welcome to the second edition of *Lost and Found.* This book was originally intended as a follow-up to my earlier book *Lost at School,* which was first published in 2008. So why write another book on the same topic? Because many of the very same educators and parents who found *Lost at School* to be helpful told me they wanted more: more instruction on using the assessment instrumentation of the model (called the Assessment of Lagging Skills & Unsolved Problems [ALSUP]), more help in using and guiding others in solving problems collaboratively, and more information on organizing and sustaining the effort to transform discipline practices and implement the Collaborative & Proactive Solutions (CPS) model in a school. Those are the ingredients you'll find in the ensuing pages. Even if you haven't previously read *Lost at School,* all of the details of the CPS model are included in this book as well.

And why publish a second edition? Because the CPS model has evolved substantially since the first edition was published in 2016. This edition reflects the most current updates.

But the most exciting aspect of this book is that you'll be hearing from some of the amazing, courageous, visionary educators who have implemented the model in their schools and classrooms and with whom I've had the incredible privilege of collaborating. They are quoted throughout each chapter by their first names; here are their full names:

Tom Ambrose, superintendent in SAU 17 in New Hampshire
Kathy Bousquet, former second-grade teacher, Central School, South Berwick, Maine
M. Scott Brinker, district behavior specialist, Groveport Madison Schools, Groveport, Ohio
Alanna Craffey, second-grade teacher, Central School, South Berwick, Maine
Nina D'Aran, principal at Central School, South Berwick, Maine
Carol Davison, district principal, human resources, Surrey, British Columbia Schools
Susan Forsely, former educational technician, Central School, South Berwick, Maine
Ryan Gleason, principal, Yarmouth, Maine Elementary School, and formerly assistant principal at Durham (Maine) Community School and Falmouth (Maine) Elementary School
Nicole Grant, teacher educator and former classroom teacher
Katie Marshall, former learning center teacher, Central School, South Berwick, Maine
Susan McCuiag, former principal at T. E. Scott Elementary, Surrey, British Columbia, and at Betty Huff Elementary, Surrey
Ryan Quinn, principal, Kennebunk Elementary School, Kennebunk, Maine
Alex Spencer, former Manhattan borough principal, Alternative Learning Centers, New York City Public Schools
Vicki Stewart, former director of communications at MSAD 35 in Maine and former principal at Central School
Brie Thomas, school counselor, Central School, South Berwick, Maine

They represent a small fraction of the many educators who have embraced the CPS model and have helped many thousands of vulnerable, at-risk students in the process.

The mission remains the same: understand and help students with concerning behaviors in ways that are nonpunitive, non-adversarial, non-exclusionary, skill building, relationship enhancing, collaborative, proactive, and—most important—*helpful.* In too many schools, those ingredients are still missing. That's why rates of detention, suspension, and expulsion are still way too high, why schools in nineteen states in the United States still employ corporal punishment, why restraint and seclusion procedures are still employed hundreds of thousands of times in schools every year, and why there are still so many kids who feel disenfranchised, marginalized, disheartened, hopeless, and *lost.* To bring them back into the fold, we need to find our way to new lenses and new practices. And this needs to be a priority for every school.

The task is not made easier by the fact that classroom teachers have been given the very strong message that their job performance and security are judged by how their students perform on high-stakes tests. Although standards can be a good thing, the obsession with tests hasn't been good for classroom teachers or administrators or parents or students with concerning behaviors, or anyone else. But, as you'll be reading, many schools have accomplished the mission despite all the obstacles.

If you're brand-new to the CPS model, many of your existing beliefs and practices may be called into question by what you read in the ensuing pages. That's OK; our knowledge of kids with concerning behaviors has expanded dramatically over the past forty to fifty years, and it turns out that a lot of what we were thinking about those kids—and doing to them—doesn't square up with what we now know about them. If you're already familiar with the CPS model, this book will take you further.

In an effort to be sensitive to different preferences, the book is written using male, female, and gender-nonspecific pronouns in alternating chapters. I've drawn on a multitude of real kids and educators I've known and worked with in the dialogues in the book, but they are composites; any resemblance to people you may know is purely coincidental (but not necessarily surprising).

I'm looking forward to spending some time with you in the next nine chapters.

Ross Greene
Freeport, Maine

CHAPTER 1

WHO AND WHY

This book is primarily focused on students whose difficulties meeting academic and social expectations at school is communicated through concerning behaviors. The ones who are flying frequently into the assistant principal's office. The ones who are on the receiving end of countless discipline referrals, detentions, suspensions, expulsions, restraints, seclusions, and (yes, in many places, still in the year 2021) paddlings. That these interventions aren't helping is made clear by the fact that they are being applied so frequently to the same students. In almost every school, 70 to 80 percent of discipline referrals are accounted for by the same fifteen to twenty students.

Those are the kids we are losing. We find them in our statistics on dropping out, teenage pregnancy, substance abuse, and incarceration. These are also very expensive kids. Placing a student in a program outside of the mainstream classroom is very costly: more than sixty-five thousand students are placed in alternative education settings every year in the United States, at a cost of an estimated $5 billion. The annual cost of incarcerating kids is even greater. So the stakes are high, both in human and financial terms.

But they're not the only ones we're losing when we don't effectively help these students. Their reasonably well-behaved classmates lose, too. There's lost learning. And there's the stress and anxiety of feeling unsafe in the presence of a peer who can be scary and may seem out of control. And these classmates also have the sense that the adults aren't exactly sure what to do or how to make things better. They may also sense that the ways in which peers with concerning behaviors are being treated are unnecessarily ostracizing and inhumane.

Classroom teachers lose as well (and we lose them, too). Those students—and their parents—are cited as a major contributing factor by many of the high number of teachers who leave the profession within the first four years. And the emphasis on high-stakes testing has caused many classroom teachers to feel like test-prep robots, which, many tell me, has taken a lot of the humanity out of the work. Legislators and school boards often aren't focused on humanity; they're focused on test scores and new initiatives and budgets and reducing referrals into special education.

We lose paraprofessionals and ed-techs as well. These staff members spend a good part of the day with kids with concerning behaviors, but frequently don't even get invited to the meetings in which those kids are being discussed. They are therefore relegated to the "winging-it" approach to intervention, along with the other people in the building—specialists such as the art, music, and physical education teachers—who work with lots of different students but often feel like they know very little about them.

"Sometimes, due to time, specialists (music, art, and so forth) and paraprofessionals can get left out of the conversation in schools. Including them in meetings is so valuable. They have so much insight, and I think we forget about that sometimes because they have such a hard schedule. They have such an important voice because they see everybody in the whole school."

—Nina, principal

Parents of students with concerning behaviors get lost, too. Those parents know a thing or two about feeling ostracized.

They often would welcome the opportunity to collaborate with school staff on making things better, but being blamed for their child's concerning behavior—despite the fact that they have other children in their families who are well behaved—makes them defensive and seldom seen. They want to trust that their child is being well treated at school, but there are many signs to the contrary. Whatever the school is doing isn't working, but the parents feel powerless to do anything about it.

We also risk losing our sense of community as a school when we don't effectively help students with concerning behaviors. Parents of the reasonably well-behaved students—the kids who are showing up ready to learn—may disparage ill-behaved classmates, often demand that those classmates are dealt with harshly and punitively, and may even ostracize the parents of those kids. They understandably want their children to learn and feel safe, but they often lose sight of what is being lost—a child who could be a valued member of the community—when those goals are pursued at the expense of that child.

Administrators, you're in the mix, too. You didn't sign up to be a police officer, but that doesn't mean you don't often feel like one. The classroom teachers who are sending kids to the office expect action and are frequently quite clear about what the action should be: powerful adult-imposed consequences, straight from the school's discipline handbook, that will finally get the message through and ensure that the well-behaved students (and their parents) know that the situation is being taken seriously. The only problem, of course, is that all those consequences aren't working. No one is more acutely aware of that than you. And there are much more effective, compassionate ways to demonstrate that the situation is being taken seriously.

“I remember my first few years as assistant principal before implementing CPS in our school. Students were lined up outside my office for various behavioral issues on a frequent basis. Since I thought of myself as the 'fix-it' person, my goal was to resolve the situation as quickly as possible. I wanted to support the teacher and help the student become more successful, but the same students, often sent from the same teachers, seemed to return over and over again. I always felt that there had to be a better way to do this. ❞

—RYAN, PRINCIPAL

Also in the mix are school psychologists, counselors, and social workers, the people who are officially on the hook for "fixing" students with concerning behaviors. It's often said that those students fall outside the expertise and responsibility of the general education classroom teacher, and therefore they fall (or are sent) into your caseload. And there are lots of 'em. And you may be covering several different buildings. And your testing load is intense. It's hard not to become overwhelmed, jaded, and burned out.

Apparently, we're talking about everyone. And that's good, because it's going to take everyone to turn things around. But when we do turn things around, everyone benefits.

So now, the question: Are the ways in which your school is assessing and dealing with students with concerning behaviors truly helping? If not, you need to find a different way.

That starts with taking a look at what you've been thinking about kids with concerning behaviors. The lenses through which you're viewing these kids will have a major influence on the stance you take toward them and the strategies you employ in your efforts to help. It's a classic case of *What you see is what you get.* What we're thinking and seeing and doing should be a reflection of the mountain of research that has accumulated over the past forty to fifty years on kids with concerning behaviors.

Here's what we've been *thinking*: kids with concerning behaviors are lacking *motivation.* Here's what the research that's accumulated over the past forty to fifty years tells us: they're lacking *skills.* And that is a game-changer.

❝ When I first learned that concerning behaviors were due to lagging skills, it was like a lightbulb went on. It's what I'd been thinking; I just never really had words for it. ❞

—KATIE, LEARNING CENTER TEACHER

Here's what we've been *doing*: we've been carefully documenting a student's concerning *behaviors*—through behavior checklists, behavior observations, functional behavior assessments (FBAs)—and we've been trying to *modify* those behaviors through administration of consequences. Here's what we should be doing instead: identifying the *problems* that are causing those behaviors and *solving* them.

And those two seismic shifts are going to change the narrative and the outcomes for a lot of kids.

As you may already know, the Collaborative & Proactive Solutions (CPS) model described in this book operates on a very important key theme:

KIDS DO WELL IF THEY CAN

This is the belief that if the kid *could* respond to problems and frustrations adaptively, he *would*. If he's not responding adaptively, he must be lacking the skills to respond adaptively. That's why he's screaming, swearing, hitting, kicking, spitting, throwing, destroying, or running out of the building. But he's not exhibiting those concerning behaviors *all* the time; he only exhibits those behaviors when there are expectations he's having difficulty meeting. So the behavior is just the signal, just the means by which the student is communicating that there's an expectation he's having difficulty meeting. If caregivers are focused only on modifying behavior, then all they're modifying is the signal. But they're not solving any of the problems that are causing the signal. So one of the most important things you can do for a student with concerning behaviors is to figure out what *skills* he's lacking. The other important thing you can do is identify the *expectations* the student is having difficulty meeting. In the CPS model, those unmet expectations are referred to as *unsolved problems*.

❝ Working in a building where behavioral incentives have been a traditional part of the culture, I often have staff members question the philosophy of extrinsic versus intrinsic motivation. Teachers would ask, 'Shouldn't students want to do well for the sake of doing well, not just to earn something?' The CPS model answers that question with a resounding *yes* with the fundamental beliefs that *kids do well if they can*, not *kids do well if they want to.* When you start with that shift in thinking, it leads you in different and more productive directions to help and support students in finding success. ”

—RYAN, PRINCIPAL

Here's another key theme, and it's related to the first:

DOING WELL IS PREFERABLE

This is the belief that human beings—including kids with concerning behaviors—have a strong preference for doing well (as opposed to doing poorly). In other words, they aren't responding maladaptively to problems and frustrations because they're seeking attention, or manipulating, or coercing us into capitulating to their wishes, or because they're lazy or unmotivated. Yet, in many schools, these characterizations are alive and well, along with the belief that a student's concerning behaviors are *working* for him.

Working? How? According to conventional notions about the *function* of behavior, concerning behavior helps a student *get* something (for example, attention) and helps him *escape* and *avoid* tasks that are tedious, challenging, uncomfortable, or scary. If those are the lenses you're wearing, then it will be your mission to prove to the student that his concerning behavior *isn't* going to work and to model and reinforce replacement behaviors that you believe will work better, typically through use of rewards and punishments.

But wait. Don't *all* of us get, escape, and avoid? If so, then the question isn't *whether* the student is getting, escaping, and avoiding, but rather *why the student is going about getting, escaping, and avoiding in such a maladaptive manner.* And now you have the answer, thanks to the mountain of research: *because he's lacking the skills to get, escape, and avoid in a more adaptive fashion.*

What skills does the research tell us kids with concerning behaviors are lacking? For the time being, we're going to sacrifice precision for efficiency: *flexibility/adaptability, frustration tolerance/emotion regulation,* and *problem solving.* Concerning behaviors typically occur when those skills are being demanded. And those skills are being demanded when (you now know this) kids (and the rest of us) are having difficulty meeting certain *expectations.* You'll be learning how to identify those lagging skills and unsolved problems in chapter 4.

You may not have known this, but educators are in one of the helping professions, right there alongside medical doctors, mental health professionals, and other helpers. Therefore, your role in the life of a student who is struggling can be summarized in one word: *helper.* There are two criteria for being an effective helper:

1. ***Helpers help.*** In other words, helpers—like medical doctors—abide by the Hippocratic Oath, which goes something like this: *don't make it worse.*
2. ***Helpers have thick skin.*** In other words, helpers don't take things personally. Although helpers are entitled to their feelings, helpers bend over backward to ensure that those feelings do not interfere with helping.

In many schools, the interventions that are still being applied to kids with concerning behaviors are making things worse. And in many schools, inaccurate beliefs about the difficulties of these students are interfering with helping.

If the lenses and interventions that are being applied to students with concerning behaviors aren't helping, then we will continue to lose those students and lots of other people in the process. Changing course—finding a different way—requires that the helpers recognize that. And then start the hard work of doing things differently.

So now one more question before the chapter ends: if the ways in which your school is assessing and dealing with students with concerning behaviors aren't helping, are you ready to begin the journey?

CHAPTER 2

OBSTACLES TO HELPING

Many of the developments and initiatives that have come down the pike in education in the last twenty to thirty years have made it much harder for educators to fulfill the role of helper.

Zero-tolerance policies are exhibit A. Those policies turned potential helpers into disciplinary robots and caused them to respond to concerning behaviors with algorithms rather than rational thought, as adversaries rather than as partners, with consequences rather than compassion and collaboration. Although some school systems have abandoned those policies, they're still alive and well in many places. Perhaps this explains why, in the United States, we still expel over twenty-five thousand students from public school annually, suspend (in and out of school) more than five million times a year (probably an underestimate), dole out countless dozens of millions of detentions and discipline referrals every year, use restraint and seclusion procedures close to one hundred thousand times a year, still apply corporal punishment over ninety thousand times a year (in nineteen states), and arrest kids at school or refer them to law enforcement two hundred fifty thousand times annually. Most of these punitive and exclusionary disciplinary actions are applied disproportionately to Black and Brown children.

"My population is 95 percent African American and Hispanic, 80 to 85 percent male, and between 25 and 50 percent special education. The fact that we have criminalized discipline in our school system—especially with students who have certain profiles—helps explain why we lose these students. School becomes a puzzle they cannot solve. There is a huge drop in suspensions after the tenth grade only because many of my students never get past their sophomore year."

—ALEX, FORMER SCHOOL PRINCIPAL

This goes without saying, but *if a school isn't using punitive, exclusionary disciplinary strategies, then it won't be disproportional in the application of these strategies.*

One of the most important doctrines governing interventions for students who receive special education in US public schools is the principle of the *least restrictive environment.* A similar doctrine—the *least toxic response*—should be applied to interventions for students with concerning behaviors. Detention, suspension, expulsion, paddling, and restraint and seclusion fall into the *most toxic* response category.

Doesn't a suspension at least give the teachers and the well-behaved students a break from students with concerning behaviors? Sure, for about three days. Then she's back, and with all of the same problems that caused the concerning behaviors that prompted the suspension in the first place. Along with, eventually, an attitude, which is what most of us would have if caregivers who were supposed to be helping continued to apply interventions that not only weren't helping but had the primary effect of pushing us away.

"Suspending kids doesn't help build a relationship with them; it says, 'We don't want you here.'"

—CAROL, PRINCIPAL

We've already touched briefly on exhibit B: high-stakes testing. When we tell teachers that their job performance and security will be based on how their students do well on high-stakes tests, we cause them to devote themselves to ensuring that students do well on high-stakes tests. Any perceived roadblocks must be removed. Where does this leave the students who are disrupting the class, interfering with the learning of their classmates, and consuming an inordinate amount of time? It leaves them removed. When they're removed, they lose learning, fall further behind, and, over time, become alienated and disenfranchised.

Classroom teachers have historically been among the most important socialization agents for children in our society. But when we force teachers to become disciplinary and test-prep robots, we make being a helper more difficult.

Using psychiatric diagnoses as the gatekeeper for services, placement, and funding also makes it harder to help. Many kids with concerning behaviors don't meet diagnostic criteria for any particular psychiatric disorder but badly need help. They don't receive the help we already know they need because they don't fit into a specific diagnostic bucket. And those diagnoses—which are just long lists of concerning behaviors thought to cluster together—are actually *distracting*, because they cause us to focus on *behaviors* rather than on the lagging skills and unsolved problems that are contributing to those behaviors.

The special education referral process often makes things harder. For many classroom teachers, a psychoeducational evaluation often feels like the only option for obtaining additional information about a student's difficulties. But the evaluation process can take a long time, and it is often geared toward determining only whether a student qualifies for special services, so the teachers are often disappointed in and underwhelmed by the information they receive. And such evaluations frequently don't pinpoint the specific expectations a student is having difficulty meeting.

And last, but definitely not least, the schedule makes it harder to help. School schedules were largely designed for academics, and if academic learning was the only activity going on in schools, we'd be good to go. But because there's a whole lot going in schools besides academics, that leaves classroom teachers with little time for a whole lot—perhaps, especially, helping the kids with social, emotional, and behavioral challenges.

By the way, the shifting sands have not only affected the field of education. Many of the societal shifts that have occurred over the past forty to fifty years have worked to the disadvantage of kids in general and kids with concerning behaviors in particular. As an example, it now takes two incomes to maintain the lifestyle that one income previously supported. As another example, the rate of kids living in single-parent homes has doubled in the last fifty years, so a lot of kids don't have the level of contact and interaction with their parents that they might have had three or four decades ago.

Yes, there are many obstacles to helping students with concerning behaviors. We can't address all of them. But, if we make the commitment, we can address enough of them to help a whole bunch of kids who would otherwise be lost.

Let's do this.

CHAPTER 3

PARADIGM SHIFT

Let's start thinking about the things you can do something about. We should start with your lenses. The lenses provided by the CPS model are encompassed by five paradigm-shifting components. In chapter 1, you were introduced to two of them: *kids do well if they can* and *doing well is preferable.* Here are the rest.

COMPONENT 3: FOCUS ON PROBLEMS, NOT BEHAVIORS

You've actually read a bit about this component already. But here's another metaphor to further the discussion: concerning behaviors are what are happening downstream; the problems that are causing those behaviors are waiting for you upstream. In the CPS model, you're focused almost exclusively on what's going on upstream.

In other words, concerning behavior is *late.* And interventions that are aimed at modifying behavior are focused on what's late.

By the time the behavior occurs, you're already in crisis *management* mode. The problems that are causing those behaviors are *early*. When you're solving problems proactively, you're in crisis *prevention* mode.

If concerning behavior is all we focus on in our discussions and meetings, then we will be led only to interventions that are geared toward modifying that behavior. And behavior modification strategies don't solve any problems.

"Everybody knows what the kid's challenging behaviors are—you can figure that out in two seconds—but you have to go deeper."

—NINA, PRINCIPAL

This shift in focus has significant implications for assessment. Many of the assessment practices employed in schools—*behavior* observations, *behavior* checklists, functional *behavior* assessments (FBAs)—are focused on a student's *behaviors*. If we're going to change our lenses, we'll also need to change our assessment practices. More on this in chapter 4.

COMPONENT 4: THE PROBLEM SOLVING IS COLLABORATIVE, NOT UNILATERAL

If we're going to focus on problems, not concerning behaviors, then we next need to think about how we're going to solve those problems. Many adults tend toward problem solving of the *unilateral* kind. This is when the adult decides on the solution and imposes it on the kid. But that's not what you're doing in the CPS model. In this model, the problem solving is of the *collaborative* kind.

The CPS model operates on a very important assumption: if you want to solve a problem with a kid—any kid, but especially the ones with concerning behaviors—you're a lot better off if you have a partner, a teammate. Who's your teammate? The student. In other words, solving problems is something you're doing *with* the student, not *to* the student. Kids—and everyone else—are a whole lot more receptive to participating in solving the problems that are affecting their lives when you're solving problems *with* them rather than doing something *to* them.

And the kid will actually participate in the problem-solving process? Just you wait. More on this in the ensuing chapters.

COMPONENT 5: THE PROBLEM SOLVING IS PROACTIVE, NOT REACTIVE

A great deal of the intervention that takes place with students with concerning behaviors occurs in the heat of the moment. But, as it relates to solving problems collaboratively, that's actually terrible (and unnecessary) timing. In the CPS model, 99 percent of intervention takes place proactively.

This theme, of course, often prompts a very important question: How can we solve problems proactively when we never know when the kid is going to exhibit concerning behavior and when the kid is so unpredictable? The answer: we actually do know when they're going to exhibit concerning behavior, and they're not unpredictable . . . if we put the hard work into identifying a student's lagging skills and unsolved problems on the front end. In schools—as well as everywhere else—timing really is everything.

Shifting from dealing with problems reactively to dealing with problems proactively can be quite paradigm shift. It may seem almost unimaginable, given how little time you have. Of course, the fact that you have so little time may speak, at least partially, to how you're currently dealing with concerning behaviors. We'll be discussing the time issue in greater detail later in the book.

UNHELPFUL LENSES

We're not quite done with your lenses yet. There are some very popular characterizations of kids with concerning behaviors that can interfere with your efforts to help students with concerning behaviors, including, but not limited to . . .

"They just want attention."

We all want attention, so this characterization isn't very useful for helping us understand why a kid is exhibiting concerning behaviors. Maybe the student is lacking the skills to seek attention in an adaptive fashion? Maybe the concerning behaviors aren't for the purpose of seeking attention at all. Along these lines, one of the most frequently recommended interventions for kids who are seeking attention maladaptively is *ignoring*. The rationale there is that ignoring will deprive the kid of the attention that is reinforcing the concerning behavior. But what if the behavior is actually communicating that there's an expectation the kid is having difficulty meeting? You won't want to ignore that.

"They just want their own way."

We all want our own way, so this statement doesn't help us understand why some kids try to get their own way in ways that are so maladaptive. Adaptively getting one's own way requires skills often found lacking in kids with concerning behaviors. And it takes two to tango: in every power struggle between a child and an adult, there's an adult who wants their own way, too.

"They're manipulating us."

This is a very popular, and misguided, characterization of kids with concerning behaviors. Competent manipulation requires various skills—forethought, planning, impulse control, and organization, among others—typically found lacking in kids with concerning behaviors. In other words, the kids who are most often described as being manipulative are those least capable of doing it well.

"They're unmotivated."

This is something that is frequently said about kids with concerning behaviors before their lagging skills and unsolved problems have been identified. But once those lagging skills and unsolved problems are identified, "unmotivated" doesn't even come close to capturing what's really going on.

"They're making bad choices."

They're probably lacking the skills needed for consistently making good choices.

TWO ROLES FOR HELPERS

Let's now think a little more about your role as a helper. Here are the two most important roles a helper can play in the life of a kid who's struggling:

1. **Figure out what skills the student is lacking and the expectations they're having difficulty meeting.**
2. **Start solving those problems,** but do it in a way—**collaboratively and proactively**—that engages kids in solving the problems that affect their lives and creates a problem-solving partnership.

These are the roles you'll be reading about for the remainder of this book.

> "I came to CPS because I hit that wall of futility and realized that no matter how many consequences I kept giving to these kids, nothing was going to change. I needed to change, and I needed to change how I was viewing them and dealing with them. It seems like we're often in a mind-set of, 'This kid is broken. This kid needs fixing. He needs a doctor.' I had to turn the mirror around and ask, 'Let's look at what *we're* doing, too.'"
>
> —Nina, Principal

Q & A

Question: But we've always used incentive programs in my building. Should we stop?

Answer: Most schools have been using incentive programs for a very long time. But when I ask school staff why they're still using incentive-based programs, the most common response they give—while simultaneously telling me that those programs aren't working for many of the kids they're trying to help—is "because it's the way we've always done it." Of course, if the way we've always done it isn't working for the kids we've always done it to, we probably ought to stop doing it and think of something better to do.

Question: Does this mean that consequences should no longer be applied to concerning behavior?

Answer: That's right. But let's distinguish between the two types of consequences—*natural* and *adult-imposed*—and consider whether either would solve the problems that are causing the concerning behaviors to which we're applying those consequences. Natural consequences—being liked or disliked, being included or excluded, feeling happy or ashamed by one's behavior, doing well or poorly on an exam—are very powerful and persuasive. They're also inevitable. Adult-imposed, "logical," "unnatural," or "artificial" consequences are often added when the natural consequences don't have the desired effect. These include punishments, such as being deprived of recess, being held after school, detention, suspension, and paddling; and rewards, such as stickers, happy faces, points, and special privileges. Adult-imposed consequences are also very powerful and persuasive. But if those very powerful, persuasive natural consequences didn't get the job done, it's hard to imagine why adding adult imposed consequences would accomplish the mission. And although natural and adult-imposed consequences might be effective at modifying a student's behaviors, they don't solve the problems that are causing those behaviors. The students who are on the receiving end of endless natural and adult-imposed consequences clearly need something else from us.

“You can't fault teachers for wanting to give kids more and more consequences. As a school leader, you have to listen to why teachers feel they need those consequences. With one teacher, she was feeling that her class was spinning out of control. And she was sort of feeling like, 'If I don't get this child under control now, I'll lose control of the whole group, and I won't get anything taught this year.'”

—NINA, PRINCIPAL

Question: Does the alternative definition of *function* mean that we should stop doing FBAs?

Answer: No, FBAs are a wonderful thing, but only when we stop coming to the automatic belief that a student's concerning behavior is *working* and that the behavior is effective at helping the student *get*, *escape*, and *avoid*. FBAs are a lot more meaningful when they are informed by lagging skills and unsolved problems. I've had way too many classroom teachers tell me that there's really no point in reading a student's FBA because all FBAs say the exact same thing. If all FBAs say the exact same thing, then those are perfunctory, boilerplate FBAs, not useful, informative, meaningful FBAs. You'll find a *meaningful* FBA—one filled with information about lagging skills and unsolved problems—in figure 3.1.

Question: We can't just do *nothing* in response to concerning behavior! Consequences at least help us feel like we're doing *something*. What should we do instead?

Answer: Not relying on adult-imposed consequences doesn't mean you're doing nothing. It means you've come to recognize the limitations of that form of intervention. There's no reason to continue doing something if that something isn't getting the job done. As for what you'll be doing instead, that's what the rest of the book is about.

AMBERVILLE SCHOOL DISTRICT
FUNCTIONAL BEHAVIOR ASSESSMENT REPORT

Name: TJ
Date of Birth: 04/29/2004
Parents:
Grade: 10
School: High School
Examiner:
Date of Report: 06/10/19

REASON FOR REFERRAL:

TJ was referred for a functional behavior assessment (FBA) by school staff due to concerns regarding a number of problems that appear to be impeding his learning, his integration into the classroom community, and the development of prosocial relationships. This FBA was conducted to 1) identify lagging skills and unsolved problems that are interfering with TJ's functioning in the school setting so that staff can understand his difficulties and so that these problems can be solved collaboratively; 2) identify and recommend possible environmental structures and supports (e.g., time, space, materials, interactions); and 3) identify and recommend appropriate strategies and supports needed to assist in implementing agreed upon solutions.

PROCEDURES USED:

Classroom Observations
Assessment of Lagging Skills and Unsolved Problems (ALSUP)
Review of records
Teacher Interview
Parent Interview
Student Plan B Conversation/Interview

RESULTS/FINDINGS:

Direct Observations:

Two time-on-task observations were conducted: the first, during Biology, revealed that TJ was on task 38% of the time in comparison to a same-age, same-sex peer who was on task 94% of the time. When TJ was on task, he was completing a lab writing assignment and copying homework assigned into his planner. When he was off-task, he was expected to listen to an article that was being read aloud and to write a short summary of the article. Overt behaviors exhibited during off-task times included walking around the classroom, talking with peers, and poking a peer with a pencil. His teacher, Ms. D., said that TJ is better able to meet expectations when he is paired with the two girls who are now his lab partners, but she is unable to pair him with these girls on all assignments. Ms. D. reported that she has to "keep a very close eye" on TJ and that this can make it hard for her to teach, and it gets "exhausting." In the second observation, TJ first walked from PE class to the lunch room. On the way he tried to interact with two other male peers but they rolled their eyes, turned their backs on him, and appeared disinterested in interacting with him. When TJ persisted, one of the boys held out his hand as if to stop TJ and said, "Dude, don't you get that we don't want you?" TJ appeared dejected and turned away suddenly. He banged into another student and growled "get out of my way." The other student backed off, and TJ went and sat alone at a table in the yard. He ate only a bit of his lunch and threw out the rest. He then went and sat with a group of girls at a table on the other side of the yard. He seemed calmer and happier with this group of girls, but noticeably darkened when the two boys he interacted with earlier passed in the hall adjacent to the yard. He then stood up and walked around a bit without any clear destination. The rest of lunch was uneventful; TJ played with a rubber ball he carried in his pocket, throwing it repeatedly against a wall by himself until the bell rang. According to the Vice Principal, Ms. Y., TJ gets into trouble at least 2–3 times per week with the peers with whom he interacted at the beginning of lunch, and sometimes it leads to him being restricted from the yard. She frequently requires that TJ stay with her at lunch time as a result.

Maladaptive Behaviors Impeding Positive School Functioning:

1. Verbal aggression (e.g., profane language, teasing other students)
2. Physical aggression (e.g., hitting, pushing, or shoving other students)
3. Dysregulated body movements (e.g., waving hands around, thrashing body, swinging back pack)

Function of Maladaptive Behaviors:
These maladaptive behaviors communicate that TJ is having difficulty meeting specific expectations, as described below. These expectations -- as documented by the *Assessment of Lagging Skills and Unsolved Problems* (ALSUP) -- are listed below.

Lagging Skills Contributing to TJ's Difficulties:
The ALSUP was completed in a meeting involving TJ's teachers and specialists. They felt that the following lagging skills applied to TJ:

Difficulty handling transitions, shifting from one mindset or task to another
Difficulty doing things in a logical sequence or prescribed order
Difficulty persisting on challenging or tedious tasks
Poor sense of time
Difficulty maintaining focus
Difficulty managing emotional response to frustration so as to think rationally
Difficulty "seeing the grays"/concrete, literal, black-and-white thinking
Difficulty taking into account situational factors that would suggest the need to adjust a plan of action
Difficulty attending to or accurately interpreting social cues/poor perception of social nuances
Difficulty appreciating how his/her behavior is affecting others

Unsolved problems precipitating challenging behaviors:
The following unsolved problems (unmet expectations) were identified during the same ALSUP meeting:

Difficulty moving from one classroom activity to the next:

- Biology to geometry
- Geometry to meeting with the school counselor
- Coming in from PE for English Literature
- Coming back from lunch to getting started on World War II project in Social Studies

Difficulty completing writing tasks, including:

- The World War II project in Social Studies
- The Shakespeare composition in English Literature
- The answers to the geometry problems in math

Difficulty working with a partner, including:

- Completing the lab report in Biology
- Preparing the class presentation on the World War II project in Social Studies with his partners

Difficulty remaining seated:

- While listening to an article that was being read aloud in Biology
- While writing a short summary of the article during on assigned mat during morning meeting

Difficulty keeping hands to self when standing in line for:

- Lunch
- PE
- School bus

Difficulty completing review sheets for homework in Biology
Difficulty getting along with Trevor and Justin during PE

These problems impede positive school functioning because:

1. TJ is unable to develop positive relationships with other students in his classroom and school community and is struggling to learn appropriate social interactions and norms.
2. This affects TJ's ability to stay regulated in class and limits his access to instruction as well as affects his ability to successfully work in groups with peers.
3. TJ's body movements distract him and his classmates and prevent him from getting the most out of instruction.

4. TJ gets sent to the office and consequently loses instructional time, thus missing out on valuable opportunities to acquire new skills and abilities.

Prior Plan B Problem-Solving Discussions:

TJ was engaged in several Plan B problem-solving conversations prior to the writing of this FBA for the purpose of gathering preliminary information about some of the unsolved problems delineated above. He identified several factors making it difficult for him to complete the World War II project in Social Studies, including the fact that writing tasks have always been difficult for him and that no mutually satisfactory solution has ever been reached to help him with this problem. As regards his difficulty getting along with Trevor and Justin during PE, he indicated that these classmates have been treating him poorly since elementary school, and that this problem has never been addressed satisfactorily.

Team estimate of need for behavior support plan:

extreme	serious	√ moderate	needing attention, early stage intervention

Factors maintaining problem behaviors:

1. For social interactions with male peers:
   a. TJ is ignored by his male friends when they do not want to interact with him and receives attention from peers when he is physically or verbally aggressive, reinforcing his negative behaviors.
   b. TJ does not have social skills strategies to talk through and figure out how to get what he wants from his peers.
   c. TJ does not have distress tolerance skills to handle not being included by his male peers.
   d. TJ does not have the ability to handle his heightened emotions so as to think clearly regarding alternative options once he feels he has been rejected.

2. For proprioceptive physical feedback
   a. TJ does not have a place (in or outside the classroom) where he can go to move his body when he feels the need for such stimulation.
   b. TJ does not have tools (in or outside the classroom) to identify when he needs proprioceptive stimulation that is less disruptive to classroom functioning, or to effectively communicate when he needs to remove himself from class if the need is over.
3. For academic tasks
   a. TJ continues to experience significant frustration on specific tasks involving writing, and this problem has been a source of frustration for him for many years. . .yet the problem remains unsolved.

Goals/Objectives of FBA:

1. Through Plan B problem-solving discussions, help TJ resolve the problems delineated above.

Teaching strategies and necessary curriculum or materials for high priority unsolved problems:

Goal 1 (Social Interactions)

- Through Plan B problem-solving conversations (individually and with the two male peers), help TJ and his peers process concerns and work toward solutions that will address the difficulties TJ and the two peers are having in interacting adaptively.
- Through Plan B problem-solving discussions, help identify the factors that are making it difficult for TJ to join interactions and maintain positive relationships with peers (e.g., when to approach others; what kinds of cues indicate he is welcome or not; ways to check for clarity regarding if he has or hasn't been rejected).

Goal 2 (Sensory Issues)

- Through Plan B problem-solving discussions, help TJ identify conditions in which he feels the need for motion or sensory stimulation and work toward solutions aimed at helping address and communicate about these needs.

Goal 3 (Academic)

- Through Plan B problem-solving discussions, determine the factors that are making it difficult for TJ to complete specific writing assignments, and collaboratively determine solutions for addressing these factors.

By whom? Teacher, classroom staff, support staff How frequently? Daily/weekly

Environmental structure and supports to be provided (Time/Space/ Materials/Interactions)

Time:

- Access materials that he can use to meet need for proprioceptive physical feedback (rough paper on his desk, a fidget, a squeezy ball, etc.).
- Calming breaks as needed

Materials:

- Plan B
- Fidgets, etc.
- Chart to memorialize solutions and agreements

Interactions:

- The vast majority of interventions -- particularly Plan B discussions -- should occur proactively rather than emergently. However, should TJ become dysregulated over an unsolved problem, the following recommendations should be applied:
  - Determine whether the expectation prompting the dysregulation was supposed to have been removed (Plan C) . . . if so, let TJ know that the expectation was placed upon him in error.

- Determine whether a solution is already in place for the unsolved problem and whether it simply isn't working; if so, let TJ know that it would be best to engage him in a Plan B discussion as soon as possible so as to revisit the problem.
- Use a calm, positive tone and reassure TJ that the problem can be solved.
- Use additional de-escalation strategies as necessary to ensure TJ's safety and that of other students.

Who will establish? Teacher, classroom staff Who will monitor? Teacher, classroom staff

Communication provisions:

Communication between teacher and parents will be facilitated by the use of the weekly log communicating how successful TJ is in solving high-priority unsolved problems.

Implementation:

A Behavior Intervention Plan (BIP) will be generated by the team —comprised of many of the actions described in the second half of this FBA—to support these goals and help improve TJ's school functioning.

____

School Psychologist

Figure 3.1 CPS-Flavored Functional Behavior Assessment

“I was skeptical about CPS. I have a very intense behavioral background. I was steeped in the whole routine of applying consequences for undesirable behavior and rewarding positive behavior. So CPS was like learning a whole new language for me. It was like discovering that the sky was purple; I didn't realize that there was another world out there. At first, I really struggled. I wanted to be able to embrace it, but it just didn't make sense. Eventually I found it productive to question my old beliefs and practices. I think having a disabled child myself, and having him go through school, helped to change my perspective. I forbade his school from giving him time-outs; I didn't want him to be punished for things related to his neurologically based condition—things that stickers and punishment weren't going to change. So

I think having my son helped me see other kids with concerning behaviors through different lenses. But one of the biggest hurdles is that even today, teachers are being trained to use carrots and sticks as their primary classroom management tools. ”

—SUSAN, EDUCATIONAL TECHNICIAN

Question: What do we say to the well-behaved kids when they observe that their behaviorally challenging classmates are being treated differently or aren't receiving the consequences that are usually applied to misbehavior?

Answer: We point out the reality. The consequences weren't working very well anyway. You're working hard on the problem and intend to keep everyone safe. Fair doesn't mean equal. In every classroom, different kids are being treated differently, according to their needs, and that approach benefits everyone, including the well-behaved students. Behavioral differences should be handled no differently than academic differences.

“ These kids who are receiving endless consequences . . . they often feel like the world is out to get them. So they project that they don't care. But they didn't get to the point of not caring overnight, so I wouldn't expect that we're going to solve all of their problems overnight either. I mean, you've got to work with them for a while. ”

—TOM, SUPERINTENDENT

Question: Isn't it important to know the cause of the student's concerning behavior? I mean, that's what we spend a lot of time talking about in our meetings.

Answer: The field of developmental psychopathology tells us that the same concerning behavior can be caused by a variety of different risk factors (a concept known as equifinality). The list of risk factors is pretty long, but includes trauma, exposure to substances in utero, premature birth, brain injury, and environmental deprivation. In many meetings, those causal factors are a primary focal point of discussion. But the reality is that we can't really establish the cause of a student's difficulties with great precision. And, often, we can't do much about those factors now anyway. What should we be talking about instead? Lagging skills and unsolved problems.

By the way, the same risk factor can give rise to a variety of different concerning behaviors (a concept known as multifinality). The list of concerning behaviors is pretty long, too, but includes behaviors that I refer to as *lucky* (for example, whining, pouting, sulking, withdrawing, crying) and *unlucky* (for example, screaming, swearing, hitting, kicking, spitting, biting, destroying, and running). You don't want to take those categories too seriously, except for one thing: caregivers are far more likely to respond with empathy, nurturance, and support with lucky behaviors than with unlucky behaviors. But, as you now know, whether lucky or unlucky, the behavior is communicating the same thing: there's an expectation the student is having difficulty meeting.

“ That's one of the biggest things that came out of implementing CPS in my school: many classroom teachers had no idea that they could have this powerful impact with kids through the relationships they were building with them and the problem-solving discussions they were having with them. ”

—SUSAN, PRINCIPAL

CHAPTER 4

THE ALSUP

Identifying lagging skills and unsolved problems is a major step forward in changing lenses and more effectively helping students with concerning behaviors. The instrument developed for this purpose is called—what else?—the Assessment of Lagging Skills and Unsolved Problems (ALSUP). The ALSUP should become the standard pre-referral, triage instrument in your building. It often obviates the need for formal testing. As you've read, it may also eliminate the need for a formal FBA (or at least provide the information needed to complete the FBA). And it's going to save you a lot of time.

The first thing to notice about the ALSUP—the most current version is called ALSUP 2020 (see figure 4.1)—is the list of lagging skills in the top section. It's not an exhaustive list of lagging skills; if we were to be exhaustive about the skills kids with concerning behaviors have been found to be lacking, the ALSUP would be ten to fifteen pages long. We don't need ten to fifteen pages to help adults recognize that lagging skills are the reason a student is responding maladaptively to problems and frustrations. Eighteen lagging skills should do the trick.

To download the blank ALSUP form and the ALSUP Guide, go to www.livesinthebalance.org/LostandFound.

ALSUP 2020
ASSESSMENT OF LAGGING SKILLS & UNSOLVED PROBLEMS

Collaborative & Proactive Solutions
THIS IS HOW PROBLEMS GET SOLVED

CHILD'S NAME ______________________ DATE __________

The ALSUP is intended for use as a **discussion guide** rather than as a freestanding check-list or rating scale. It should be used to identify specific lagging skills and unsolved problems that pertain to a particular child or adolescent.

LAGGING SKILLS

This section will help you understand why the child is responding so maladaptively to problems and frustrations. Please note that these **lagging skills are not the primary focal point of intervention**. In other words, you won't be discussing the lagging skills with the student, nor will you be teaching most of the skills explicitly. The primary targets of intervention are the unsolved problems you'll be documenting in the next section.

☐	Difficulty maintaining focus	☐	Difficulty seeing "grays"/concrete, literal, black & white, thinking
☐	Difficulty handling transitions, shifting from one mindset or task to another	☐	Difficulty taking into account situational factors that would suggest the need to adjust a plan of action
☐	Difficulty considering the likely outcomes or consequences of actions (impulsive)	☐	Inflexible, inaccurate interpretations/cognitive distortions or biases (e.g., "Everyone's out to get me," "Nobody likes me)"
☐	Difficulty persisting on challenging or tedious tasks	☐	Difficulty attending to or accurately interpreting social cues/poor perception of social nuances
☐	Difficulty considering a range of solutions to a problem	☐	Difficulty shifting from original idea, plan, or solution
☐	Difficulty expressing concerns, needs, or thoughts in words	☐	Difficulty appreciating how his/her behavior is affecting others
☐	Difficulty managing emotional response to frustration so as to think rationally	☐	Difficulty starting conversations, entering groups, connecting with people/lacking other basic social skills
☐	Chronic irritability and/or anxiety significantly impede capacity for problem-solving or heighten frustration	☐	Difficulty empathizing with others, appreciating another person's perspective or point of view
☐	Sensory/motor difficulties	☐	Difficulty handling unpredictability, ambiguity, uncertainty, novelty

UNSOLVED PROBLEMS

Unsolved problems are the specific expectations a child is having difficulty meeting. The wording of an unsolved problem will translate directly into the words that you'll be using when you introduce an unsolved problem to the child when it comes time to solve the problem together. Poorly worded unsolved problems often cause the problem-solving process to deteriorate before it even gets started. Please reference the ALSUP Guide for guidance on the four guidelines for writing unsolved problems.

SCHOOL/FACILITY PROMPTS:
Are there specific tasks/expectations the student is having difficulty completing or getting started on?
Are there classmates this student is having difficulty getting along with in specific conditions?
Are there tasks and activities this student is having difficulty moving from or to?
Are there classes/activities the student is having difficulty attending/being on time to?

HOME/CLINIC PROMPTS:
Are there chores//tasks/activities the child is having difficulty completing or getting started on?
Are there siblings/other children the child is having difficulty getting along with in specific conditions?
Are there aspects of hygiene the child is having difficulty completing?
Are there activities the child is having difficulty ending or tasks the child is having difficulty moving on to

REV 102020

livesinthebalance.org

LIVES IN THE BALANCE

Figure 4.1 The ALSUP (Assessment of Lagging Skills and Unsolved Problems) 2020

In the bottom section is where you'll be writing (or typing, if you're using the editable, fillable format) unsolved problems, using the prompts in that section. Again, an unsolved problem is an expectation the student is having difficulty reliably meeting.

The fact that there is a place to check off the lagging skills can sometimes cause people to think that the ALSUP is a checklist or rating scale. It's neither. Caregivers who work with kids with concerning behaviors are frequently asked to check and rate too much. And, of course, what we're busy checking and rating is *concerning behavior* (the signal). Then we tabulate our ratings and count our checks so that we can calculate a total score. Then we compare the student's total score to normative data for kids of the same age, grade, or gender. All in the quest for what has become the holy grail of assessment: a *percentile* that will somehow communicate to us whether the student needs our help. A student doesn't need a percentile to need your help. If he has unsolved problems, he needs your help.

Instead, the ALSUP is a *discussion guide*—a guide for discussing a student's lagging skills and unsolved problems. Checklists don't help the different adults who are working with a student have a shared set of lenses, but a discussion should. Checklists don't help those adults speak the same language; a discussion should. Checklists don't persuade people to change their lenses; a discussion should.

The ALSUP helps us focus on the things we can actually do something about rather than on the things about which we can do little or nothing. In meetings in which the ALSUP is the discussion guide, *the sole focus is on lagging skills and unsolved problems.*

USING THE ALSUP

Let's consider the format of meetings in which the ALSUP is used. First, everyone in the meeting is given a *blank* copy of the ALSUP, though one participant should take the lead on checking off lagging skills and recording unsolved problems. It's far less productive to have participants fill out the ALSUP prior to the meeting, because that's not conducive to a discussion. And we really do want to have a discussion.

The student is not involved in the ALSUP meeting. That's because we want school staff to speak freely and because there are things we don't want the student to hear. The student will never be aware of all of the lagging skills and unsolved problems that are identified. He'll only be aware of the high-priority unsolved problems that are going to be the focal point of problem-solving discussions.

I don't generally recommend having parents in the first ALSUP meeting. Again, we want school staff to speak freely. Although it's a very good idea to get on the same page with parents about lagging skills—the failure to do so often causes parents and educators to jump prematurely to *solutions*, a topic on which they're likely to disagree because they haven't yet achieved a consensus about lagging skills—that's better saved for a second meeting. Plus, with a few important exceptions, the expectations a kid is having difficulty meeting at home are likely to be quite different from the unsolved problems the kid is having difficulty meeting at school. School staff are on the hook for dealing with the expectations the student is having difficulty meeting at school. Parents are on the hook for dealing with the expectations the kid is having difficulty meeting at home. The exceptions are unsolved problems on which there is *overlap* between home and school: for example, homework; coming to school on time; coming to school at all; coming to school well-clothed, well-fed, and well slept; and separating from parents to come into the building. On those unsolved problems, school staff and parents will need to work together in collaborating with the student on solutions.

“We had to move away from the idea that it's the parents' responsibility to handle problems that are occurring at school. It became clear that we—the people working with the kid at school—were the ones best positioned to help make changes in kids' lives at school.”

—Kathy, teacher

The discussion begins at the top of the ALSUP by identifying the lagging skills that apply to the student. Checking off lagging skills is the easy part of using the ALSUP. Deciding whether or not to check off a particular lagging skill isn't something to obsess over, nor is it a democratic process. If one or two people in the ALSUP meeting feel that the student is lacking the skill, check it off. If none of the meeting participants feel that the student is lacking that skill, move on to the next one. It shouldn't take long to complete the lagging skill section, perhaps about five minutes. That's about ten to twenty seconds per lagging skill. By the way, it's not unusual for adults to check off virtually all of the lagging skills for a particular student.

Now, you might be thinking that students with concerning behaviors are lacking other skills that aren't listed on the ALSUP, especially those related to academic tasks. Yes, there are quite a few lagging skills that may contribute to a student's difficulties in reading, or writing, or doing math, or spelling. But *the lagging skills on the ALSUP account for why he's responding so poorly to the frustration he experiences when he's presented with or trying to work on those academic tasks.*

After the lagging skills section is completed, you're ready to identify unsolved problems, using the appropriate prompts. The first prompt for schools and facilities is *Are there specific tasks/expectations the student is having difficulty completing or getting started on?* If the math teacher says, "Well, he's not completing the double-digit division problems on the worksheet in math," then *Difficulty completing the double-digit division problems on the worksheet in math* is an unsolved problem. If the English teacher says, "He's refusing to write the paragraphs in Writer's Workshop," then *Difficulty writing the paragraphs in Writer's Workshop* is an unsolved problem. Come up with as many unsolved problems as possible for that prompt before you move on to the next prompt. You don't need to write the same unsolved problem twice, even if one of the other prompts causes that unsolved problem to come to mind again.

Identifying and wording unsolved problems is the hard part of completing the ALSUP. There are four guidelines involved in writing unsolved problems. These guidelines make it harder to write unsolved problems, but they're worth the added difficulty, for they increase the likelihood that the student will participate in the process of solving the problem. That's because *the wording of the unsolved problem on the ALSUP translates directly into the words that will be used to introduce the problem to the child when it comes time to solve it together.* Poorly worded unsolved problems can stop the process dead in its tracks. Writing unsolved problems isn't going to be hard forever; it's only going to be hard until you become comfortable with the four guidelines.

GUIDELINES FOR WRITING UNSOLVED PROBLEMS

1. **The wording of the unsolved problem should contain no concerning behaviors.** People who are unfamiliar with the ALSUP are often tempted to write concerning behaviors (hitting, swearing, screaming) in as the unsolved problems, probably because they've been focused on those behaviors all along. Not anymore. Concerning behaviors are not the unsolved problems; the unmet expectations that are causing the behaviors are the unsolved problems. Remember, behavior is just the signal—it's *downstream.* The problems causing the behavior are *upstream.* So we're leaving the behavior out of the wording of unsolved problems. In other words, we're not going to write an unsolved problem as follows: *Gets upset and runs away when told to stay in place in the line from the classroom to lunch.* "Gets upset and runs away" is the concerning behavior . . . it's gone, replaced by the word *Difficulty.* So the correct wording would be *Difficulty staying in place in the line from the classroom to lunch.*

A verb almost always follows the word *difficulty*. For example, *Difficulty completing, Difficulty getting started on, Difficulty getting along with, Difficulty sitting next to* . . . and so forth. Verb selection is the hardest part of writing an unsolved problem. To make it easier, you'll find a list of sample unsolved problems, each containing a different verb on the ALSUP Guide (figure 4.2).

ALSUP GUIDE Collaborative & Proactive Solutions
THIS IS HOW PROBLEMS GET SOLVED

The **Assessment of Lagging Skills and Unsolved Problems (ALSUP)** is a discussion guide created to assist caregivers in identifying a child's lagging skills and unsolved problems. Lagging skills provide caregivers with new lenses. Rather than viewing a child's difficulties as attention-seeking, manipulative, coercive, unmotivated, lazy, or limit testing, lagging skills provide more accurate, productive, actionable lenses.

INSTRUCTIONS FOR IDENTIFYING LAGGING SKILLS:

How hard could it be to check off lagging skills? Not that hard, but here are a few important reminders:

- Go in order...you don't want to miss anything.
- Don't spend time hypothesizing or theorizing about causal factors (why the student is lacking these skills)...you can't establish cause with any level of precision, and your time will be better spent identifying lagging skills and unsolved problems
- Don't spend any time talking about the child's behavior either...the behavior is simply the way children communicate that there are expectations they are having difficulty meeting
- Checking off a lagging skill is not a democratic process and shouldn't take more than 3-5 seconds each. If any caregivers in the meeting think the lagging skill applies to the child, check it off.
- While lagging skills provide you with new lenses -- a worthy goal -- lagging skills are not the primary targets of intervention. The unsolved problems you'll be identifying are the primary targets of intervention. If you solve those problems collaboratively and proactively, the child's skills will be enhanced.

INSTRUCTIONS FOR IDENTIFYING UNSOLVED PROBLEMS:

An unsolved problem is ***an expectation a child is having difficulty meeting***. Writing unsolved problems is harder, because the wording of the unsolved problem on the ALSUP is going to translate directly into the words that you're going to use to introduce the unsolved problem to the child when it comes time to solve the problem together. As such, there are four guidelines for writing unsolved problems:

They should contain no reference to the child's *challenging* behaviors. Since you won't be talking with children about their behavior, there's no need to include the behavior in the wording of the unsolved problem. Instead, almost all unsolved problems begin with the words Difficulty, followed by a verb (a variety of verbs are shown in the examples below as well). So you wouldn't write *Screams and swears when having difficulty completing the word problems on the math homework*...instead write *Difficulty completing the word problems on the math homework.*

They should contain no adult theories. So you wouldn't write *Difficulty writing the definitions to the spelling words in English... because his parents were recently divorced.*

They should be split, not clumped (so you wouldn't write *Difficulty getting along with others* but rather *Difficulty getting along with Trevor on the school bus in the morning.*

They should be specific. To make an unsolved problem as specific as possible, there are two strategies:

- Include details related to *who, what, where,* and *when*
- Ask *What expectation is the child/student having difficulty meeting?*

The above guidelines -- and a variety of sample verbs -- are embodied in the following examples (they're grouped based on setting, but the verbs apply across settings):

SCHOOL/FACILITY:

- Difficulty getting started on the double-digit division problems in math
- Difficulty completing the map of Europe in geography
- Difficulty participating in the discussions in morning meeting
- Difficulty moving from choice time to math
- Difficulty ending computer time to come to circle time
- Difficulty walking in the hallway between classes
- Difficulty raising hand during Social Studies discussions
- Difficulty keeping hands to self in the lunch line
- Difficulty lining up for the bus at the end of the school day
- Difficulty remaining quiet when a classmate is sharing his or her ideas in English
- Difficulty waiting for his turn during the four-square game at recess
- Difficulty retrieving Geography notebook from locker before Geography class

HOME/CLINIC:

- Difficulty getting out of bed at 7 am in the morning to get ready for school on weekdays
- Difficulty going to church on Sundays
- Difficulty taking turns when playing chess with brother
- Difficulty sitting next to sister at dinner
- Difficulty putting the dishes into the dishwasher after dinner
- Difficulty taking the trash out on Tuesdays
- Difficulty brushing teeth before going to bed at night
- Difficulty ending Xbox at 8 pm
- Difficulty making bed before school on weekday mornings

There are also a variety of verbs that should be avoided, including *accepting, appreciating, staying calm, asking for help, listening, paying attention, focusing, considering, understanding, persisting, controlling.*

REV 102020

LIVES IN THE BALANCE

livesinthebalance.org

Figure 4.2 The ALSUP Guide

Why is this an important guideline? Because if you mention a kid's concerning behavior when you're trying to solve a problem with him, he's likely to become defensive or think he's in trouble. And if one or both of those things happen, he's going to be far less receptive to participating in the discussion. And, because we're trying to collaborate, we very badly want him to participate in this discussion. Second, we want to make it crystal clear to the people in the ALSUP meeting that the concerning behavior is not the unsolved problem; again, the unmet expectation causing the behavior is the unsolved problem. That way, they'll stop talking about the behaviors and start talking about the expectations the student is having difficulty meeting.

2. **The wording of the unsolved problem should contain no adult theories.**

If we want to spend our meeting time talking about the things about which we can do something, we're going to talk a lot less (if at all) about our theories and explanations related to the cause of the student's behavior. And we're certainly not going to include our theories in the wording of our unsolved problems. In other words, we wouldn't write *Difficulty sitting next to Thomas during circle time because her parents are going through a very difficult divorce.* Anything that comes after the word *because* is pretty much guaranteed to be a theory and is left out of the unsolved problem.

Why? First—don't take this personally—because *our theories are often wrong.* We think they're right, but they're wrong a lot more often than we think they are. Again, when you're using the ALSUP, there's no pressure to explain anything. You're focused solely on identifying lagging skills and unsolved problems. Second, tossing a theory at the kid in the midst of introducing an unsolved problem—"*I've noticed you're having difficulty sitting next to Thomas during circle time because your parents are going through a very difficult divorce"*—is likely to confuse the kid and make it very difficult for him to figure out what information you're seeking (*"Are they asking me about sitting next to Thomas or about the divorce?"*). Many will simply say, *"I don't know"* or not respond at all.

“ These days, if I'm sitting in a meeting and all they're doing is theorizing and talking about behavior and telling stories, I get frustrated and bored. I feel like, 'This is so pointless. We're not talking about anything that we can change.' All the theorizing can *feel* productive because we're talking about the kid, we're making connections, we're talking about the student's life. But then you realize there's no point in talking about that stuff. Let's talk about things we can actually do something about. ”

—KATIE, LEARNING CENTER TEACHER

Along these lines, I've begun recommending that adults strive for something I call *assumption-free living*. The instant you feel you already know what's making it difficult for a student to meet a particular expectation, get rid of that assumption as quickly as possible. It's just a distraction. Plus, as you'll soon see, your top source of information on what's making it hard for a student to meet a particular expectation is the student.

But wait . . . wasn't a lot of your training centered on helping you figure out what could be making it hard for a student to meet certain expectations and helping you come up with strategies for remediating those difficulties? Was all that training for naught? No, not for naught, but if you apply strategies for remediating a student's difficulties before actually finding out the true nature of those difficulties, you're going to miss the mark. A lot.

“ You know, in the old days, when we'd meet about a kid, all the people who worked with the kid in the school would get together to talk about everything we knew about the kid and then brainstorm solutions. And the teacher would choose two or three to try. Now we know someone was missing from the problem-solving process: the student. Now we only really talk about lagging skills and unsolved problems in our meetings, because we can't come up with solutions without knowing the kid's concerns and without involving the kid in the solution. ”

—KATHY, SECOND-GRADE TEACHER

3. **The wording of the unsolved problem should be split, not clumped.**
   What does this mean? Here are some examples of clumped unsolved problems:
   - Difficulty getting along with others
   - Difficulty reading
   - Difficulty staying safe
   - Difficulty following directions
   - Difficulty listening
   - Difficulty writing

   The problem is that these unsolved problems are too global. The student may be having difficulty getting along with many different people (and for different reasons), may be having difficulty reading many assignments (and for different reasons), may be having difficulty following many different directions (again, for different reasons), and may be having difficulty doing the writing on many different assignments (yes, for different reasons). If the wording of the unsolved problem refers to many different unmet expectations, it will be virtually impossible for the student to respond.

   Let's use *Difficulty writing* to clarify further. If we use the words, *"I've noticed you're having difficulty writing"* to introduce an unsolved problem, then we're asking the student to think about *all* of the different assignments he's having difficulty writing and *all* of the different reasons he's having difficulty writing them. That's often asking for too much sorting through, so such wording greatly increases the likelihood of the student responding with

"I don't know." Plus, although it's tempting to believe that the student is having difficulty on all of the writing assignments for the *exact same reason,* that won't actually be the case most of the time. So we're going to *split* the unsolved problem by being precise about the specific individual writing tasks and assignments the student is having difficulty completing. Let's say she's having difficulty writing the term paper in social studies, difficulty writing the definitions to the spelling words in English, and difficulty writing the answers to the word problems in math. Those are three separate unsolved problems.

Our motto is *split early; maybe you can clump later . . . but if you clump early, you'll never find out.* This means that when it comes time to solve problems, we're going to talk to the student about *one* of the writing tasks or assignments she's having difficulty completing (say, *difficulty completing the term paper in social studies*). Because it's been split, we've greatly increased the likelihood that she will participate in the discussion and provide us with information. After we're through gathering information from the student about that single writing task or assignment, we can then ask her if what we now understand about the reasons she's having difficulty completing the term paper in social studies also helps us understand the difficulty she's having in writing the definitions to the spelling words in English. The answer is either yes or no. If the answer is no, it's good that we split the unsolved problem, because the student's difficulties on the two writing assignments are different. But even if the answer is yes, splitting was still a smart play, because the student would have been less likely to talk about it if it had been clumped.

One of the biggest concerns people have about splitting unsolved problems is that it makes the list of unsolved problems very long. But if the list of unsolved problems is very long, that's the reality. If there are many expectations the student is having difficulty meeting, then we're not doing her or ourselves any favors by pretending that the list is shorter than it really is. *The real favor is that, finally, at long last, all of the expectations the student has been having difficulty meeting for a very long time have been identified.* Plus, even if the list is lengthy, you're not going to be working on all of the unsolved problems at once anyway. We'll discuss prioritizing later in this chapter.

4. **The wording of the unsolved problem is as specific as possible.** There are two strategies that will help with this:

Strategy 1: asking "W" questions (*who, what, where,* and *when,* but not *why*)

Strategy 2: inquiring about the expectation the student is actually having difficulty meeting

Let's bring these strategies to life with some examples. Let's say a meeting participant proposes *Difficulty being impulsive* as an unsolved problem. Don't write that in yet! It's too global. So now let's use our strategies.

Where is she impulsive? (Strategy 1)

"She's impulsive during social studies."

What's going on during social studies when she's being impulsive? (Strategy 1)

"She always calls out answers without raising her hand during social studies discussions."

That unsolved problem just became a lot more specific after just two applications of Strategy 1. We're almost ready to log that unsolved problem on the ALSUP. But it needs a little additional refining, because there's still a concerning behavior (calling out answers) in there. Let's take *calling out answers* out of the unsolved problem and insert the word *difficulty.* Now we have an unsolved problem (*Difficulty raising hand during social studies discussions*) that contains no concerning behavior, contains no adult theories, is split, and is specific.

You might be thinking that "raising hand" is a behavior, and you'd be right, but it's not a *concerning* behavior (for example, screaming, swearing, hitting). It's the expectation that the student is having difficulty meeting, so it's fine.

Here's another example. Let's say someone in the meeting says that a student "has a lot of rage." Not good, right? That's either a concerning behavior or a theory, but it's not a specific unsolved problem (yet). So let's use our strategies:

Where does she have a lot of rage? (Strategy 1)

"Recess."

What's going on during recess—and with whom—that makes you say she has a lot of rage? (Strategy 1)

"She always kicks her best friend, Teresa, when they disagree about the rules in the four-square game."

That's a lot more specific. We're almost ready to write that unsolved problem down on the ALSUP. There's only one remaining issue: there's still a concerning behavior in there (kicking). So let's take *kicking* out and put the word *difficulty* in. Now what do we have? *Difficulty agreeing with Teresa on the rules in the four-square game during recess.* Good! Well, not good that she's having difficulty agreeing with Teresa on the rules in the four-square game during recess, but good that we've worded that unsolved problem in a way that increases the likelihood that the student will help us understand what's making it difficult to meet that expectation.

Here's another. Let's say a meeting participant proposes *Difficulty with the word* no as the unsolved problem. Don't write that in! The word *no* is not the unsolved problem. What caregivers are saying *no* about could be the unsolved problem. Let's use our strategies:

What are you saying no about? (Strategy 1)

"I'm saying, 'No, you can't go to the bathroom eighteen times during every math period.'"

OK, well, going to the bathroom a lot during math period is the concerning *behavior*... but what expectation is he having difficulty meeting during math period? (Strategy 2)

"Oh, he's having difficulty using the software on the computer during math."

Difficulty using the software on the computer during math is the unsolved problem.

Here are some examples of unsolved problems that do not meet the guidelines. Try to figure out which guideline the unsolved problem isn't meeting.

Difficulty moving from one activity to the next.

If you recognized that this is clumped, well done! To split it, we'd need to be more explicit about the specific activities the student is having difficulty moving from and to, even if that means writing ten different unsolved problems. Strategy 1 (*What activities is she having difficulty moving from and to?*) should help. Some examples of split unsolved problems that might be identified in this instance:

Difficulty moving from English to math.
Difficulty moving from recess back into the classroom.
Difficulty moving from the resource room back to the classroom for math.

Again, although it would be tempting to think that the student is having difficulty moving from all assignments, classes, and activities to the next for the exact same reason, that's unlikely to be true.

Here's another:

Difficulty moving from a preferred activity to a less preferred activity.

Clumped, yes? But this unsolved problem also includes a very common theory (preferred and less preferred). We're a lot better off just documenting the specific activities the student is having difficulty moving from and to (using Strategy 1) without worrying about which is preferred or unpreferred:

Difficulty moving from lunch to the resource room.
Difficulty coming from the bus into the classroom in the morning.

Here's another one that needs some refining:

Difficulty completing difficult assignments.

This, you may have noticed, is clumped and may also contain a theory. What we really want to identify are the specific assignments the student is having difficulty completing (using Strategy 1):

Difficulty completing the word problems on the worksheet in math.
Difficulty getting started on the definitions in English.
Difficulty getting started on the geography project in history.

And one more:

Difficulty treating others with respect when he's upset.

Now, this one is pointing us downstream (*when he's upset*). To make this unsolved problem more specific, we'd need to ask about the problems that are causing the student to become upset (Strategy 1):

Difficulty finding someone to sit with at lunch.

Difficulty finding someone to sit with on the school bus.

Difficulty when he thinks the kids are cheating during the basketball game at recess.

How do you know that last one isn't a theory? Whenever a potential theory is raised in an ALSUP discussion, you'll want to ask the informant, *"How sure are you?"* If the answer is, *"Not very sure,"* it's probably a theory. But if the informant responds, *"He [the student] has told me that's why he gets upset at recess,"* it's not a theory.

In other words, information that's already been provided by the student is usually good protection against adult theorizing. But it's not infallible. A long time ago, I asked a four-year-old girl why she was exhibiting concerning behavior (that's a question I wouldn't ask anymore), and she responded, "I do it for negative reinforcement." This turned out to be a regurgitation of something adults had told her.

> “If you jump into solving problems and you haven't really done the ALSUP first, you're kind of putting the cart before the horse.”
>
> —Carol, Principal

Here's some more:

Difficulty arriving to class on time.

Clumped. What class(es)?

Difficulty doing things on the first request.

Clumped. What things?

Difficulty not lying.

Pure concerning behavior. What's the student lying about? Some people might be tempted to change this to *Difficulty telling the truth,* and that might feel like a step in the right direction, but it's still clumped, and we'd still need to know what the student is having difficulty telling the truth about. If the student is having difficulty telling the truth about whether she's completed her lab reports in science, then *Difficulty not lying* and *Difficulty telling the truth*—which are downstream—would be replaced by *Difficulty completing her lab reports in science.*

Also, you want to avoid unsolved problems that include the word *not* whenever possible, especially because concerning behavior almost always comes after the word *not.* So *Difficulty not pushing people in the lunch line* would be altered to the actual expectation the student is having difficulty meeting: *Difficulty keeping hands to self in the lunch line.* And *Difficulty not calling kids mean names on the bus* would be altered to *Difficulty speaking kindly to John and Trevor on the school bus.*

Here's one more:

Difficulty getting off the computer when I tell her to.

The *difficulty getting off the computer* part is fine, but the *when I tell her to* part isn't, mostly because it's not specific enough.

So let's ask some questions:

When are you telling her to get off the computer?

"At the end of choice time."

And what expectation is she having difficulty meeting when she doesn't turn off the computer at the end of choice time?

"She's supposed to be going to math."

Always math?

"Yes, math is always after choice time."

So she's having difficulty turning off the computer at the end of choice time to go to math?

"Yes!"

Enough examples? I was thinking the same thing. OK, here's an example of an ALSUP reflecting well-worded unsolved problems (figure 4.3).

ALSUP 2020
ASSESSMENT OF LAGGING SKILLS & UNSOLVED PROBLEMS

Collaborative & Proactive Solutions
THIS IS HOW PROBLEMS GET SOLVED

CHILD'S NAME ______________________ DATE __________

The ALSUP is intended for use as a **discussion guide** rather than as a freestanding check-list or rating scale. It should be used to identify specific lagging skills and unsolved problems that pertain to a particular child or adolescent.

LAGGING SKILLS

This section will help you understand why the child is responding so maladaptively to problems and frustrations. Please note that these **lagging skills are not the primary focal point of intervention**. In other words, you won't be discussing the lagging skills with the student, nor will you be teaching most of the skills explicitly. The primary targets of intervention are the unsolved problems you'll be documenting in the next section.

☐	Difficulty maintaining focus	☑	Difficulty seeing "grays"/concrete, literal, black & white, thinking
☑	Difficulty handling transitions, shifting from one mindset or task to another	☑	Difficulty taking into account situational factors that would suggest the need to adjust a plan of action
☑	Difficulty considering the likely outcomes or consequences of actions (impulsive)	☐	Inflexible, inaccurate interpretations/cognitive distortions or biases (e.g., "Everyone's out to get me," "Nobody likes me)"
☑	Difficulty persisting on challenging or tedious tasks	☐	Difficulty attending to or accurately interpreting social cues/ poor perception of social nuances
☑	Difficulty considering a range of solutions to a problem	☑	Difficulty shifting from original idea, plan, or solution
☐	Difficulty expressing concerns, needs, or thoughts in words	☑	Difficulty appreciating how his/her behavior is affecting others
☑	Difficulty managing emotional response to frustration so as to think rationally	☐	Difficulty starting conversations, entering groups, connecting with people/lacking other basic social skills
☐	Chronic irritability and/or anxiety significantly impede capacity for problem-solving or heighten frustration	☑	Difficulty empathizing with others, appreciating another person's perspective or point of view
☐	Sensory/motor difficulties	☐	Difficulty handling unpredictability, ambiguity, uncertainty, novelty

UNSOLVED PROBLEMS

Unsolved problems are the specific expectations a child is having difficulty meeting. The wording of an unsolved problem will translate directly into the words that you'll be using when you introduce an unsolved problem to the child when it comes time to solve the problem together. Poorly worded unsolved problems often cause the problem-solving process to deteriorate before it even gets started. Please reference the ALSUP Guide for guidance on the four guidelines for writing unsolved problems.

SCHOOL/FACILITY PROMPTS:
Are there specific tasks/expectations the student is having difficulty completing or getting started on?
Are there classmates this student is having difficulty getting along with in specific conditions?
Are there tasks and activities this student is having difficulty moving from or to?
Are there classes/activities the student is having difficulty attending/being on time to?

HOME/CLINIC PROMPTS:
Are there chores//tasks/activities the child is having difficulty completing or getting started on?
Are there siblings/other children the child is having difficulty getting along with in specific conditions?
Are there aspects of hygiene the child is having difficulty completing?
Are there activities the child is having difficulty ending or tasks the child is having difficulty moving on to

Difficulty moving from homeroom to Chinese class
Difficulty keeping hands to self in the hallway between Geography and World History
Difficulty keeping hands to self in the hallway between World History and Math
Difficulty getting to school on time
Difficulty turning in vocabulary homework in Chinese
Difficulty putting away iPhone in homeroom
Difficulty getting along with Geoff during football in physical education
Difficulty completing the reading assignments for homework in American Literature
Difficulty getting along with Ricky on the school bus
Difficulty getting along with Tucker at lunch
Difficulty copying the information from the white-board during Biology
Difficulty writing homework assignments into planner

REV 102020

livesinthebalance.org

LIVES IN THE BALANCE

Figure 4.3 A Completed ALSUP

HELPFUL MEETINGS

Aside from identifying lagging skills and unsolved problems, what do we hope happens in an ALSUP meeting? As mentioned, we hope lightbulbs flicker on as the following happens:

- Participants come to appreciate that the student is, indeed, lacking a lot of skills. Good, that's a great step away from thinking the student is lacking motivation.
- Participants come to appreciate why interventions that have been focused primarily on motivation haven't been working. Motivation wasn't the issue all along.
- Participants who have been treating the student in a harsh, adversarial, exclusionary, punitive manner may start to feel some regret now that they understand what's really getting in the way for the student.
- Participants come to recognize that concerning behaviors occur only in the context of specific unsolved problems and are therefore highly predictable.
- Participants recognize that if unsolved problems are predictable, they can be solved proactively rather than emergently.
- Participants also come to recognize that if those problems were to be solved, they wouldn't cause concerning behaviors anymore.

“Having worked with many teachers to support them in completing an ALSUP, I am always amazed at their reaction the first time we sit down and do it together. As they check off lagging skills, you can observe and feel them developing a deeper understanding of why some of the concerning behaviors are occurring. Once that process begins, they are much more able to focus on the problems instead of the symptoms. They truly start to understand the student, and the empathy and approach that results from that understanding are critical to reaching the student and helping her solve problems collaboratively.”

—RYAN, PRINCIPAL

The alternative, of course, is to continue discussing concerning behaviors, diagnoses, and things about which nothing can be done, in which case participants will continue to leave meetings feeling that they can do nothing to help the student, and also possibly feeling that the meeting was a complete waste of time.

> “We struggled with the ALSUP in the beginning. We were taking way too long. There was still way too much hypothesizing and theorizing going on in our meetings, and it was really hard to get away from that because that's what the teachers wanted to talk about. But once we got rid of all that chatter, we could usually get an ALSUP done in fifty minutes.”
>
> —SUSAN, PRINCIPAL

PRIORITIZING

It's not uncommon for school staff to feel completely overwhelmed by the sheer number of lagging skills and unsolved problems. But there's a silver lining to all those lagging skills and unsolved problems: *at least you now know what they are.* In other words, *not* knowing about them is far more overwhelming than knowing about them. And you're not going to be trying to solve all of those unsolved problems at once anyway, tempting as that might be. Indeed, trying to solve all of those problems at once is the best way to ensure that none of them gets solved at all.

You're going to have to prioritize. Which unsolved problems are going to be solved first, and which are we setting aside for now?

Before we talk about that, here's another reason to feel less overwhelmed by that long list of unsolved problems: now that you've identified them, they can be solved *proactively.* When unsolved problems remain unidentified, you're still stuck trying to deal with them emergently and reactively, and that's just bad timing (and also a lot less effective). Now you don't have to wait until the student disrupts the class before you try to solve the problem that causes the disruption; you can do it in advance because the problem (and the disruption) are predictable. In other words, you're no longer responding to one incident after another (an approach captured by the well-known maxim related to chickens with their heads cut off). You're solving the problems that are causing those incidents, and now you know what those problems are. Your head is very much on.

And what about all those lagging skills you've checked off? Don't they have to be taught? Well, yes and no. Yes, enhancing those skills would be a very positive development. But you're actually not going to be teaching the vast majority of skills on the ALSUP in a direct or explicit manner *because there's no proven technology for doing so.* True, some of the skills—some basic social skills and language processing and communication skills—can be taught explicitly. But the vast majority of skills are going to be enhanced *indirectly*, by solving problems collaboratively and proactively. Put another way, *when you're solving problems collaboratively and proactively, you're simultaneously (but indirectly) enhancing the student the skills that will help him respond more adaptively to problems and frustrations.* More on this later in the book.

So your primary targets of intervention are the unsolved problems. Which ones should you prioritize? First and foremost: any that are causing *safety issues.* If there are no safety issues, go with the unsolved problems that are causing concerning behaviors with the *greatest frequency* or those that are having the greatest *negative impact* on the student's life or the lives of others. But don't obsess over prioritizing; getting started with the process of solving problems collaboratively and proactively is more important than splitting hairs over which specific unsolved problems to start with. Can the student help you decide which unsolved problems to prioritize? Sure, why not?

How many unsolved problems should you target initially? No more than three. Any more than that, and both you and the student will be working on too many things at once and no problems will get solved. What are you doing with the rest? You're setting them aside, at least for now. Unsolved problems that have been removed from the agenda won't set in motion concerning behaviors. More on this in later chapters, too.

How do you keep track of everything? With another instrument, called the Problem-Solving Plan (figure 4.4). This instrument provides a convenient mechanism for listing the problems that are presently prioritized for a student, designating the person who's

Figure 4.4 Problem-Solving Plan (Plan B Flowchart)

taking primary responsibility for solving each problem with the student, and tracking progress in solving them. Once a problem is solved, it is removed from the Problem-Solving Plan and another problem from the ALSUP takes its place. (See figure 4.5 for a sample filled-out Problem-Solving Plan.)

By the way, who's the ideal person to be solving the problem with the student? *The person whose expectation the student is having difficulty meeting.* That's probably the classroom teacher, or the specialist, or perhaps the paraprofessional or ed-tech.

But that's *not* the school counselor, or school psychologist, or school social worker. And it's not the principal or assistant principal. But aren't those the people we've been sending kids to all along? Yes, but those people—though they may have the best of intentions—can't solve problems they know nothing about. And that's why the CPS model has a pretty stellar track record of dramatically reducing or eliminating discipline referrals . . . and all the disciplinary actions that take place after disciplinary referrals.

> To download the Problem-Solving Plan form, go to www.livesinthebalance.org/LostandFound.

Some schools have found that the Problem-Solving Plan eventually takes the place of the old Behavior Plan. The Behavior Plan is focused on the wrong thing (behaviors); the Problem-Solving Plan is focused on the right thing (the problems that are causing those behaviors).

In the hustle and bustle of the school day, problems (and students) can get lost in the shuffle. Under such circumstances, the problems never get identified and solved. The ALSUP and Problem-Solving Plan keep that from happening. They keep things organized. They make problem solving systematic and proactive. They save time. They ensure that problems—and kids—don't slip through the cracks.

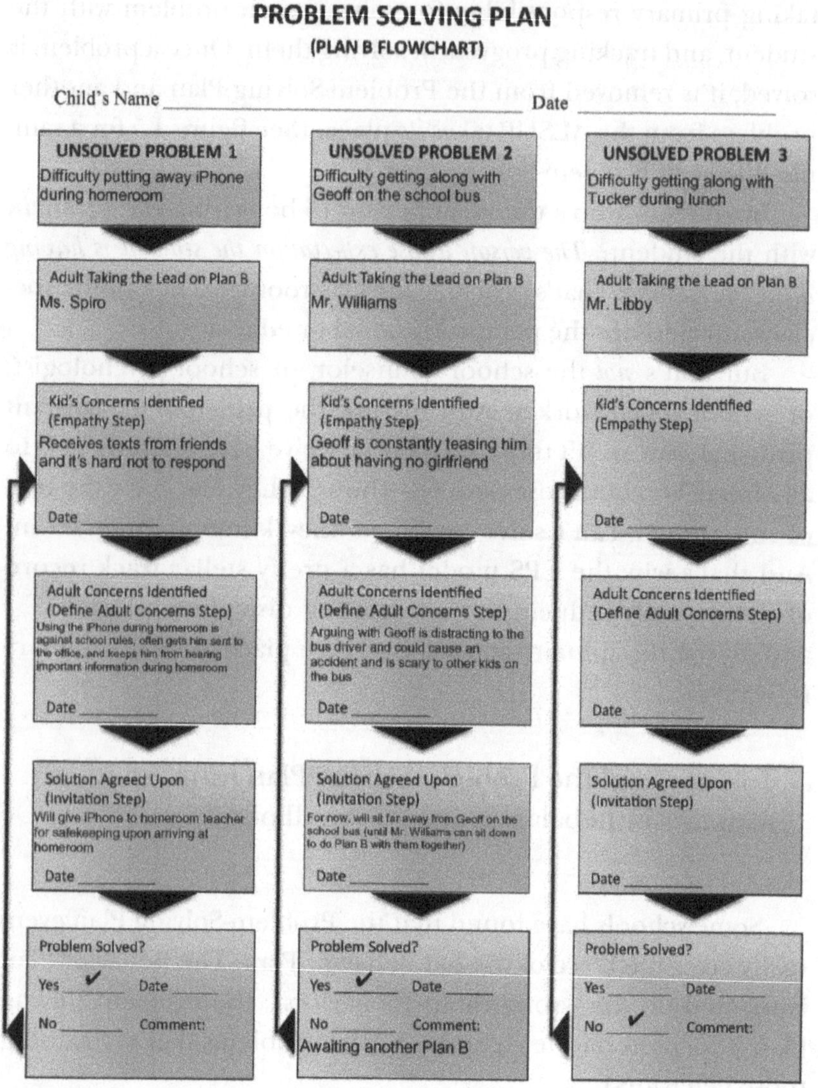

Figure 4.5 A Completed Problem-Solving Plan

Q & A

Question: What if I have thirty students in my classroom and five or ten of them have concerning behaviors? Do I need an ALSUP for all five or ten?

Answer: That would be ideal, just to help you organize the effort. Helping ten students simultaneously is a daunting task in and of itself, and it's even more daunting if you're not going about it in a systematic, planned manner. Remember, all those unsolved problems didn't get there overnight, and you're not going to get them solved overnight, either. So, rather than chronically putting out brushfires—let's face it, that's why those problems got stacked up in the first place—you'll know what problems you're trying to solve (and which ones you're setting aside, at least for now) with each student. Slowly but surely, you'll not only see progress with each student but also in the general functioning of your class as a whole.

Question: If a kid only has a few unsolved problems, do I need to complete the entire ALSUP, or can I just start solving problems?

Answer: Start solving problems. But if a student has a long list of unsolved problems, identifying and prioritizing are critical. Otherwise you run the risk of working on everything at once and of working on problems that aren't your top priorities.

Question: In my school, we don't really meet together as a group very often. Is the ALSUP something I can complete on my own?

Answer: Yes, you could complete the ALSUP on your own. But it would be better to find ways to get together with all the people in the building who interact with the same student. That way, everyone's on the same page. Otherwise, the left hand won't know what the right hand is doing.

Question: What if it takes more than one meeting to cover all the lagging skills and unsolved problems?

Answer: That'll be time well spent, especially when we consider how much time is being spent on the student because we haven't yet identified her lagging skills and unsolved problems.

Question: Isn't there something to be said for letting staff members vent about students in a meeting?

Answer: Sure, for about two minutes. But if the entire meeting is spent on venting—if staff members never get around to the information that's been missing (lagging skills and unsolved problems)—then they'll still be venting in the next meeting . . . and the next.

Question: On previous iterations of the ALSUP, weren't the lagging skills divided into categories?

Answer: Yes, quite some time ago, the lagging skills were divided into five categories: executive skills, language processing and communication skills, emotion regulation skills, cognitive flexibility skills, and social skills. But I found that the categories were doing more harm than good. First, there's so much overlap among the categories that it's actually a bit artificial to treat them as discrete entities. Second, I found that caregivers were counting the number of checks within a category as a means of prioritizing, when it's actually not lagging skills that are being prioritized; it's unsolved problems that are being prioritized. Third, it's the specific lagging skills—not the categories—that really help caregivers understand what's making it hard for a kid to respond adaptively to problems and frustrations.

In the version of the ALSUP that immediately preceded the ALSUP 2020, the lagging skills were used as prompts for helping caregivers think of unsolved problems. But we found that created a lot of confusion and took more time. We find that the ALSUP 2020 is less confusing and takes far less time to complete.

Question: Aren't lagging skills and unsolved problems kind of negative? Isn't it important to focus on the student's strengths, too?

Answer: It's great to focus on a kid's strengths in addition to his lagging skills and unsolved problems. Remember, though, that it's not the strengths that are contributing to concerning behaviors; it's lagging skills and unsolved problems.

And although talking about lagging skills and unsolved problems may seem negative, it's often a vast improvement over what caregivers have been saying about the kid. Interestingly, the CPS model is often characterized as a strength-based approach . . . probably because it includes no strategies that are punitive, adversarial, or exclusionary. Even some interventions calling themselves "positive" are still relying on adult-imposed consequences (rewards) that are aimed at modifying behavior. But the failure to achieve an anticipated reward can cause concerning behaviors just as much as a punishment can. We often forget that both rewarding and punishing are cut from the exact same bolt of cloth.

Question: In talking about unmet expectations, is it also useful to think about whether the expectations are realistic for the student?

Answer: Yes! That's a very important part of the discussion. Unrealistic expectations are often a major precipitant of concerning behaviors. Why would we want to place an expectation on a student that he can't reliably meet?

Question: I can see completing the ALSUP and Problem-Solving Plan in the usual meetings that take place in my school. But where do you think I'm going to find the time to solve all of those problems?

Answer: There are some pockets of time throughout the school day that can be devoted to problem solving if we're systematic about it. Sometimes I refer to this as "buried time." Before school, after school, during lunch, during recess, during prep time, when the rest of the class is busy working on something—these are all times that can be devoted to problem solving. And, as you'll read in chapter 8, many schools have committed to carving out specific times every day to solving problems with students. One thing is quite certain: not solving problems takes up a lot more time than solving them.

"What struck me as I began using the ALSUP was how much we adults were focused on our theories about the factors that were causing our students to have difficulty. We'd compete with each other to see who had the most insight about the kid. We were totally focused on things like gang affiliation, family problems, protective services, suspension histories, probation cases, and psychiatric diagnosis. It's not that these things are irrelevant, it's just that the more we theorized, the more powerless we felt to help the student make any progress. When we started learning how to use the ALSUP, we discovered the unsolved problems that had been causing great difficulty for our students—and that had remained unsolved—for a very long time. We discovered that we'd been focused on the wrong things."

—ALEX, FORMER SCHOOL PRINCIPAL

CHAPTER 5

THE PLANS

Thanks to the ALSUP, we've now identified the information that was missing about a student with concerning behaviors. We have new lenses (lagging skills, not lagging motivation) and have made a seismic shift in focus (from concerning behaviors to the problems that are causing those behaviors). There may be a lot of things you can't change in your school, but those aren't two of 'em.

Now we're ready to starting thinking about another thing we can change: how to solve problems with students. There are basically three options for dealing with unsolved problems, and they're called Plan A, Plan B, and Plan C. You're really only using two of these Plans in this model: B and C. Plan A is in there primarily as a reference point, because it's still quite popular. But you're almost never using Plan A in this model.

Plan A refers to solving a problem *unilaterally.* This is when adults decide on the solution to a problem and impose the solution on a kid, often accompanied by adult-imposed consequences. Plan A is far and away the most popular way that adults handle problems or unmet expectations with kids, and not only in schools.

Its popularity notwithstanding, Plan A can actually be counterproductive in many ways and, for a variety of reasons, isn't the ideal approach to solving problems. More on that in a few paragraphs.

Plan C involves *setting aside* a particular unsolved problem, at least temporarily. Although many caregivers worry that Plan C is the equivalent of giving in or giving up, it's not. There's no such thing as giving in or giving up in the CPS model. There is, as you've read, such a thing as *prioritizing* in the CPS model, and, as you now know, prioritizing is actually a crucial aspect of organizing our efforts to help students with concerning behaviors.

Plan B involves solving a problem *collaboratively*. It's Plan B that helps you create a partnership with the student. It has the greatest potential for durably solving problems, reducing the concerning behaviors that are being caused by those problems, and enhancing the skills the student is lacking.

By the way, if a student is reliably meeting a given expectation, you don't need a Plan. It's not an unsolved problem. The Plans are purely for the expectations a student is having *difficulty* meeting.

The Plans provide a nice framework—a shorthand—for considering how we're approaching unsolved problems. Let's take a closer look at each option.

PLAN A

If a kid isn't meeting a given expectation, one way to solve the problem is by imposing a solution. The words *"I've decided that . . ."* tell you that's exactly what you're doing, as in, "Because you're having difficulty keeping your hands to yourself in line when we're walking to recess, *I've decided that* you'll be walking next to me in the back of the line from now on." Or "Because you're having difficulty completing your math during math period, *I've decided that* you're not going out for recess until the math is done."

Notice, *having an expectation* and *imposing a solution* aren't the same thing. In the first example, keeping hands to self when in line walking to recess is the expectation the student is having difficulty meeting; the imposed solution is walking next to the teacher. In the second example, completing the math work during math period is the expectation the student is having difficulty meeting; staying in from recess until the math is done is the imposed solution. So don't get confused: using Plan A to solve a problem is not the same thing as having an expectation. Put a different way, *just because you have an expectation doesn't mean you're using Plan A.* Put another way, *just because you're not using Plan A doesn't mean you don't still have expectations.*

That's important, because one of the common reactions to the CPS model—especially the part of the model that discourages the use of Plan A—is that it involves abandoning all expectations. It doesn't involve anything of the sort. You still have expectations, lots of 'em. How you go about handling *unmet* expectations—unilaterally or collaboratively—is where the rubber meets the road. (This probably wouldn't be a bad time to point out that most students with concerning behaviors are meeting way more expectations than they're not.)

There are quite a few drawbacks with using Plan A to solve problems. Among them: *Plan A greatly heightens the likelihood of concerning behavior in kids who are lacking the skills to handle problems and frustrations adaptively.* No one especially enjoys have other people impose solutions on them. It's frustrating. Equally frustrating is a second drawback: solutions arrived at through Plan A are *uninformed.* Such solutions are based on adult *theories* about the cause of the problem, but not on any information from the intended beneficiary of the solution: the kid. With Plan A, you're not seeking that information. And that's why solutions arrived at through use of Plan A tend not to work very well or for very long.

A third and related drawback is that Plan A *does not involve the student in solving the problems that affect her life.* Why would we want to exclude students from participating in solving the problems that affect their lives? Isn't the ability to solve problems going to be a crucial skill for doing well in The Real World?

Fourth, Plan A does not lend itself to an adult-child problem-solving partnership. In fact, Plan A typically has the effect of pushing kids away. Why would we want to push kids away when we could be working in partnership with them?

Plan A involves power; power causes conflict. Plan B involves collaboration; collaboration brings people together.

Can you get away with Plan A with "ordinary" kids? Perhaps. But why would you want to? The drawbacks involved in using Plan A with kids with concerning behaviors are equally applicable to "ordinary" kids, except that ordinary kids are less prone to exhibit concerning behaviors in response to Plan A. Don't we want to be partnering with well-behaved kids, too? We'll consider those questions more thoroughly in chapter 9.

Plan A has historically been a very popular way of solving problems with kids. And that, at least partially, explains why we're still losing so many of our most vulnerable kids. Why is Plan A still so popular in so many schools? Because in a lot of schools very little thought has been given to solving problems in a different way. But not your school. Not anymore.

PLAN B

Any problem that can be solved using Plan A can also be solved using Plan B. The primary difference between the two Plans is that with Plan A, problems are being solved unilaterally and with Plan B, problems are being solved collaboratively. But that's a massive difference.

Plan B helps adults clarify and understand what's making it hard for a student to meet a particular expectation. Plan B also helps the kid understand the adult's concerns about the problem. And Plan B helps adults and kids work together, as partners, toward mutually satisfactory solutions so that both parties' concerns are addressed, the student is involved in solving the problems that affect her life, the problem gets solved durably, the behaviors that were being caused by the problem subside, and skills are enhanced.

"I remember after many Plan B discussions, teachers would say, 'I had no idea that's what was going on for that student. I never would have guessed that in a million years.'"

—CAROL, PRINCIPAL

There are two ways to use Plan B: *emergently* and *proactively*. On first hearing about Plan B, adults often come to the erroneous conclusion that the best time to use Plan B is at the precise moment that a kid begins to have difficulty meeting an expectation. But that's Emergency Plan B, and the timing is actually not ideal because the kid may already be upset or heated up and because, if you're a teacher, you've got a lot of other things going on in your classroom at that moment. Few of us do our clearest thinking or resolve difficult problems when we're already upset, so crisis *management* is not your best long-term strategy; crisis *prevention* is far preferable. Because unsolved problems are highly predictable, you don't have to wait until a problem has popped up yet again to start solving it. As you've read, problems don't just pop up. The goal is to solve them before they occur. That's Proactive Plan B. You'll learn about the three steps of Plan B in chapter 6.

"Proactive Plan B is definitely preferable, especially when you are just starting to have discussions with a student. It's a lot easier to build a relationship that's built on trust and empathy when you're not in the heat of the moment."

—KATHY, TEACHER

> See a teacher engage in basic, Proactive Plan B with his student Charlie. Go to http://livesinthebalance.org/LostandFound.

PLAN C

As you've read, Plan C involves setting aside a given unsolved problem, at least temporarily. As you've also read, Plan C is central to the process of prioritizing. Recall that students with concerning behaviors usually have quite a few unsolved problems, and it won't be possible to solve them all at once. Some unsolved problems will need to be set aside so that both the student and her caregivers are more "available" to work on higher-priority problems. Expectations that have been removed won't cause concerning behaviors because they've been eliminated for now. Not forever, for now.

There are also *emergent* and *proactive* forms of Plan C. The latter form is again preferable. If you've already used the ALSUP to identify the wide array of unsolved problems that are causing concerning behaviors, and if you've already decided on high and low priorities, then you're well positioned to use Proactive Plan C.

Proactive Plan C often involves coming up with an interim plan with the student. This is a plan for what things are going to look like while the problem is removed. Here's what that might sound like: "Max, you know how we're working on helping you get caught up on that English project you fell behind on? And we're also trying to work on the difficulties you're having getting to school on time. And we've also been trying to find a way to get you caught up on your science lab reports. We're working on a lot of things right now. I'm thinking we should hold off on working on that geography report you've been struggling with until we get some of these other problems solved. Let's think of what you're going to be doing while the rest of the class is working on their geography reports." You haven't solved the problem; you've just come up with a plan for removing it for now.

And here's what Emergency Plan C sounds like:

TEACHER, WITH AN EXPECTATION: *Class, it's time to get to work on your English projects.*

STUDENT: *I'm not doing my English project.*

TEACHER, USING PLAN C: *OK.*

The classroom teacher can get the rest of the class started on the English project and then check in with this student to gather information about her (apparently) sudden refusal to work on the project. Then the teacher can decide whether this problem is a high priority right now; if it is, the teacher would handle the problem (proactively) with Plan B. If it's not, the teacher would set the problem aside for now, perhaps by proactively discussing with the student how best to do that. But because this probably isn't the first sign of trouble on the English project, a more proactive approach was probably possible in the first place.

Does this mean you're supposed to drop all your expectations so a kid won't exhibit concerning behaviors? No, it doesn't mean that at all. But, again, it is very productive to set aside lower-priority expectations so that you and the student aren't overwhelmed trying to solve too many problems at once.

“As a school moves in this direction, it's important to let teachers know—and reassure them—that you're not throwing the baby out with the bathwater. There are still going to be basic expectations and rules and procedures in your school for maintaining order. But you're primarily starting with those children for whom you can clearly see that the old system is not working. So reassure teachers that they're not being asked to completely give up some things in order to try something that's going to take a while to put in place and master.”

—Carol, Principal

Q & A

Question: I'm a classroom teacher, and I really do feel that Plan B is best left to the mental health staff.

Answer: You may be selling yourself short. If you work in a school, you solve problems with students all the time. Now we're just formalizing the process a little and making it collaborative and proactive. So helping kids solve the problems that affect their lives isn't, and shouldn't be, solely the responsibility of the mental health staff. The reality is—and this will become clear once you've read about the three steps of Plan B—that those problems can't really be solved without you.

Question: Aren't there some things a student just has to do?

Answer: There certainly are expectations you feel very strongly that a student should meet. And many caregivers believe that Plan A is the clear choice if they feel really strongly about a student meeting a particular expectation. But it's not. The importance of an expectation is not the determining factor in using Plan A or Plan B. The decisive factor is whether the problem will be best and most durably solved unilaterally or collaboratively. In all likelihood, Plan A has already been deployed—many times—to solve a particular problem with a student. The fact that the problem is still unsolved tells you what Plan you should be using instead.

“Having worked in education for over twenty-three years, I have used Plan A, Plan B, and Plan C at different times and with students in all grade levels, K–12. There is no question that, in my experience, Plan B is the most durable, lasting way to support students in successfully solving the problems that school can present for them. Other strategies are ‘quick fixes’ and may last for a short time, but as educators, if we really want to help our students in the most meaningful way, our time is best spent using Plan B.”

—Ryan, Principal

Question: Are there some students who are so volatile and unstable that academics need to be de-emphasized until things are calmer?

Answer: Absolutely. Some kids simply aren't “available” for academic learning until headway has been made on the non-academic challenges that may be impeding learning. In such instances, academics may have to take a backseat until progress occurs on these challenges. Plunging forward with academics when a kid is bogged down with other challenges is usually an exercise in futility.

Question: So, just making sure I'm clear here: simply having and voicing an expectation is not the same thing as Plan A, right?

Answer: Right. This is a common point of confusion. Simply voicing an expectation—for example, *"Class, it's time to come in from recess"*—is not Plan A. If you impose a solution to an expectation a student is having difficulty meeting—for example, *"Matt, because you're having difficulty coming back into the classroom from recess, I've decided you're not going out for recess anymore"*—that's Plan A.

Question: So if my expectation is being met, I don't need a Plan?

Answer: Right. You only need the Plans for unmet expectations.

Question: Isn't Plan A the only way to hold kids accountable for their actions?

Answer: Definitely not. For many caregivers, holding a kid accountable for her actions simply means making sure she pays the price for her concerning behavior. That's an extremely narrow definition. If a kid is participating in Plan B, identifying and articulating her concerns, taking yours into account, and working toward a realistic and mutually satisfactory solution, she's most assuredly being held accountable. The belief that Plan A is the only way to hold a kid accountable is completely misguided and has contributed to unnecessarily poor outcomes in way too many kids.

Question: Should I still be using consequences for concerning behavior—even if I don't think they're working—so that the other kids know I'm taking the concerning behavior seriously?

Answer: The other kids don't need you to use consequences to know you're taking the problem seriously. They need to see that you've got a handle on the lagging skills and unsolved problems of their classmate with concerning behaviors and that, slowly but surely, her concerning behaviors are decreasing in frequency, intensity, and duration. *You don't improve your credibility by continuing to intervene in a way that isn't working or is making things worse.*

Question: Should I reward a kid for successfully participating in Plan B?

Answer: I generally recommend against it. The effects of Plan B—finally having one's concerns heard and identified, making headway on getting problems solved, learning new skills, resolving difficulties without conflict or concerning behavior—are far more rewarding (and far more important for you and the kid to focus on) than any extrinsic reward you might offer.

Question: So I guess I don't need my sticker chart anymore.

Answer: Perhaps not.

“I think a lot of adults are used to a model of communication where they lead, and the student does what they say, and then they get results. And Plan B reverses that paradigm. In this way, there's a lot of overlap between current practices in classroom instruction—such as universal design—and the philosophy of CPS. They're very closely related, and I think that that's a big shift. Those teachers who struggle the most with best practice in classroom instruction also struggle with what I would consider to be best practice in managing behavior . . . which is to solve problems collaboratively and proactively.”

—TOM, ASSISTANT SUPERINTENDENT

CHAPTER 6

SOLVING PROBLEMS TOGETHER

There are three steps involved in solving a problem collaboratively: the Empathy step, the Define Adult Concerns step, and the Invitation step. In this chapter, you'll be reading quite a bit about each step. Even if you're already familiar with the three steps, you'll probably find information in this chapter that takes you even further.

THE EMPATHY STEP

The Empathy step is where you'll be gathering information from a student about what's making it hard for them to meet a particular expectation. The kid is your primary source of information on that (I can't think of anyone who would be better qualified). Your mission in the Empathy step is to demonstrate to the student that you're really interested in and curious about those concerns. Thanks to the ALSUP and Problem-Solving Plan, you'll be doing that proactively most of the time.

The process of information gathering and understanding begins with an introduction to the unsolved problem. The introduction usually begins with the words *"I've noticed that . . ."* and ends with the words *"What's up?"* In between, you're inserting an unsolved problem. The introduction is made much easier—and, as you know, the likelihood that the student will respond is much greater—if you stick with the guidelines for writing unsolved problems you read about in chapter 4. Here are some examples of what the introduction would sound like, using some unsolved problems from prior chapters:

"I've noticed that you're having difficulty moving from English to social studies. What's up?"

"I've noticed that you're having difficulty moving from recess back into the classroom. What's up?"

"I've noticed that you're having difficulty completing the word problems on the worksheet in math. What's up?"

"I've noticed that you're having difficulty getting started on the geography project in history. What's up?"

Pretty straightforward so far, yes? Before we get to the hard parts, let's review a few points. First, you're not teaching any lessons in the Empathy step. Actually, you're not teaching lessons in *any* of the three steps. You're not being judgmental, either. You're also not saying many of the standard things adults say in response to kids' concerns. So you wouldn't respond to *"I don't like sitting next to Alberto"* with *"Oh, come on, he's not so bad!"* You wouldn't respond to *"The double-digit division problems are too hard for me"* with *"Oh, you'll be fine . . . we just need some more effort here."* And you wouldn't respond to *"I don't want to work with Tina on the Galileo project"* with *"Part of growing up is learning to work with people we don't like."* These are responses that cause kids to feel (often accurately) that their concerns are being ignored, disregarded, dismissed, or diminished. They also cause kids to stop talking. Then you don't obtain the information you need about what's making it hard for the student to meet a given expectation, you don't have a problem-solving partner, and the problems don't get solved.

Some adults have never considered it especially important to gather information about and understand what's making it hard for a kid to meet a particular expectation. That's why many kids—perhaps most, unfortunately—are accustomed to having their concerns go unidentified, unheeded, and unaddressed. After all, we adults often think we *already know* what's getting in the kid's way on a given problem, which may help explain why we often don't put much energy into finding out. As you've read, the bad news is that, quite often, our assumptions about kids' concerns are way off base. That's why our solutions—which are based on those assumptions—often don't solve the problem. It's not your job to know what's getting in the kid's way; it's your job to know how to find out.

> "So much of what we do as educators is assess the situation and decide on a solution . . . that's what teachers are accustomed to doing. And what we've learned is that we're not always accurate in what we assume to be the reasons behind why kids do things. Having those conversations with the kids has been a huge eye-opener. The essence of solving problems collaboratively is that the student has voice and choice in the situation. Look at the process. First we listen to them. We gather information. It's about listening, but it's also about asking the right questions. And then the adult shares his or her concerns, and then the two work together to solve problems. That parallels a lot of the cutting-edge work on academic instruction these days. So I've been lucky to see this kind of unique connection between CPS and very progressive, research-based, modern instruction."
>
> TOM, SUPERINTENDENT

Another reason adults tend to blow past kids' concerns is that we have concerns of our own, which we're eager to express. And often we've already decided on a solution anyway, one that addresses only our own concerns and that we're busy imposing.

Those are habits that we'll need to break.

Now on to the hard parts. After you ask, *"What's up?"* one of five things is going to happen:

Possibility 1: The kid says something.
Possibility 2: The kid says nothing or *"I don't know."*
Possibility 3: The kid says, *"I don't have a problem with that"* or *"I don't care."*
Possibility 4: The kid says, *"I don't want to talk about it right now."*
Possibility 5: The kid becomes defensive and says something like, *"I don't have to talk to you"* (or worse).

Let's make sure you're well prepared for each of these possibilities.

Possibility 1: The Kid Says Something

If, after the problem is introduced, the student starts talking, that's good. Now you need to keep them talking, because their initial response is unlikely to provide you with a clear understanding of what's making it hard for them to meet a given expectation. You're going to need to probe for more information. The probing process—called *drilling for information*—is actually pretty hard for many adults, especially in the beginning, mostly because they're not sure what to say. Difficulty with drilling causes many Plan B ships to run aground, thereby causing many Plan B captains to abandon ship. The good news is that there are some strategies to help you master the drilling process so that the Plan B boat stays afloat.

First, notice that the word is *drill*, not *grill*. The primary goal of drilling is to *clarify*, whereas grilling tends to be an act of intimidation or a sign that you anticipate that the student won't be forthcoming or will lie. Your goal is to demonstrate to the student that your attempt to understand what's getting in the way isn't fake or perfunctory. You're really curious . . . *you really want to understand.*

Second, *drilling* is not the same thing as *talking*. There are educators who frequently talk to (or at) their students, but they never achieve a clear understanding of students' concerns on specific unsolved problems. Drilling is much harder—and much more productive—than simply talking.

The following drilling strategies should help in the Knowing What to Say Department:

Drilling Strategy 1: Reflective Listening (Accompanied by Clarifying Questions or Statements)

This is where you're simply mirroring or repeating back whatever the student just said to you. Let's say you inquired about a student having difficulty sitting next to their classmate, Alberto, during circle time. If the student responds with, "I just don't like it," your response would be, *"Ah, you just don't like it."* Then you'd add a clarifying question or statement, such as *"How so?"* or *"I don't quite understand"* or *"I'm confused"* or *"Can you say more about that?"* or *"What do you mean?"*

If this sounds a little basic, maybe so. But reflective listening is your default drilling strategy. It's the strategy you're going to be using most often. It's the strategy to use when you're not sure which strategy to use. It helps kids feel heard. It helps kids feel understood. It clarifies and validates their concerns. And it keeps them talking. You could ask for nothing more from a drilling strategy. If you're in the midst of the Empathy step and you're not sure what to say or which drilling strategy to use, reflective listening is always a safe bet.

Drilling Strategy 2: Asking "W" questions (*Who, What, Where, or When*)

These questions are another good way to demonstrate that you're really listening and need additional information. Examples: *"Who's been giving you a hard time on the school bus?" "What's making it hard for you to complete your science homework?" "Where/when is Kyle teasing you?"* Remember, drilling is about gathering information, and W questions are a straightforward way to do so. Notice that there's another W question—*Why?*—that you should not be asking very often; that question often elicits a *theory*, and usually one that the child inherited from an adult.

Drilling Strategy 3: Asking about the Situational Variability of the Unsolved Problem

Here's what this strategy might sound like: *"So, help me understand how you're able to do the math homework sometimes and sometimes you can't."* Or *"So, sometimes you're on time for school and other times you're not. Help me understand that."*

The fact that the student meets a given expectation sometimes (but not reliably) often leads adults to jump to the conclusion that the kid can meet the expectation *when they feel like it,* and that the kid doesn't meet the expectation when they *don't* feel like it. Actually, that conclusion is just proof that adults haven't yet asked the kid why they're able to meet the expectation sometimes and not others.

The reality is that there may be nuanced, subtle differences between seemingly identical expectations that explain the inconsistency. Rather than jump to conclusions related to poor motivation—"*I know she can do the math when she wants to! She did it yesterday!*"—you'd be better off seeking clarification from the student. Remember, when you're drilling, you're off the hook for mind reading or figuring things out on your own.

Drilling Strategy 4: Asking the Student What They're *Thinking* in the Midst of the Unsolved Problem

This is an outstanding drilling strategy. *"So, when you're sitting at your desk trying to do the double-digit division problems, what are you thinking?"* Notice, you're not asking the kid what they're *feeling.* It's not that asking a student what she's feeling is a crime; it's just that the answer (happy, sad, frustrated, embarrassed, bored) won't generally provide you with the information you're seeking about what's making it hard to meet a given expectation. Also notice that you're not asking the kid what they *need* . . . that question is more likely to prompt the kid to offer up a *solution* rather than a *concern,* and you're not ready to start thinking about solutions until the Invitation step.

Drilling Strategy 5: Breaking the Unsolved Problem Down into Its Component Parts

Most unsolved problems have multiple components. For example, coming into the classroom to get started with the school day has different components (hang up your coat, take off your snow boots, sit down at your desk, start your morning reading assignment, and so on). And getting ready to go home at the end of the day has multiple components, too (reviewing homework assignments, packing up your backpack with the necessary materials for homework, putting on snow boots and coat, going to the school bus, and so on). But kids sometimes need help identifying those components so that they can tell which component is causing them to struggle:

TEACHER, INTRODUCTION: *I've noticed that it's been difficult for you to get ready to go home at the end of the school day. What's up?*

STUDENT: *I don't know.*

TEACHER: *Do you want to think about it a little?*

STUDENT, AFTER THINKING: *I really don't know.*

TEACHER: *Would it help if we thought about the different parts of getting ready to go home at the end of the school day?*

STUDENT: *OK.*

TEACHER: *Well, first, you have to look at your homework sheet so you can figure out what materials you're going to need for homework that night. Is that hard?*

STUDENT: *No.*

TEACHER: *So you're not having any difficulty looking at your homework sheet so you can figure out what materials you're going to need for homework that night?*

STUDENT: *No.*

TEACHER: *OK, the next thing you need to do is get all the materials you're going to need into your backpack. Is that part hard?*

STUDENT: *Yes.*

TEACHER: *It is? What's hard about it?*

STUDENT: *I can't always find everything I'm going to need.*

TEACHER: *What's hard about finding everything you need?*

STUDENT: *Sometimes I work with Mrs. Cassidy in a different room, and sometimes I leave stuff in her room. And sometimes I'm not sure if the stuff I need is in my locker, because I might have left it somewhere else. And sometimes Tim asks if he can borrow my books, and sometimes he doesn't give stuff back.*

TEACHER: *I think I understand.*

Good. That's better than not understanding.

Watch an administrator practice drilling strategies with a student having trouble in some of her classes. Go to http://livesinthebalance.org/LostandFound.

Drilling Strategy 6: Making a Discrepant Observation

This involves making an observation that differs from what the student has said about a particular unsolved problem. Here's what that might sound like: *"I know you're saying that you and Felicia are getting along fine these days, but yesterday at recess you two weren't getting along very well at all."*

The discrepant observation is the riskiest (in terms of causing the child to stop talking) of all the drilling strategies. That's because many kids—perhaps especially those frequently accused of lying—misinterpret a discrepant observation as an accusation of dishonesty. Fortunately, you're not accusing them of lying; you're simply pointing out that your observation differs from theirs. Just because your experience of reality differs from the student's doesn't mean they're lying. They're entitled to their reality.

Drilling Strategy 7: Tabling (and Asking for More Concerns)

This is where you're metaphorically shelving some concerns the child has already articulated so as to make it easier for them to think of other concerns. You're not dismissing the earlier concerns; you're just putting them on the back burner temporarily so as to clear space for consideration of other possible concerns.

Example: *"So if you didn't leave things in Mrs. Cassidy's room, and if you knew whether the things you need for homework were in your locker, and if Tim was giving you back the things he borrowed . . . would there be anything else that would make it difficult for you get ready to go home at the end of the day?"*

Drilling Strategy 8: Summarizing (and Asking for More Concerns)

This is where you're summarizing concerns you've already heard about in the Empathy step and then asking if there is anything else making it hard for the child to meet the expectation. This is the recommended strategy to use before moving on to the Define Adult Concerns step, just to make sure there are no other concerns.

Example: *"Let me make sure I understand everything you've said. It's hard for you to ride on the school bus because it's too loud, and because they're making you sit three to a seat so it's really crowded, and because you never get to sit on the aisle, and because Steve is picking on you and the bus driver always blames you. Is there anything else that's hard for you about riding on the school bus?"*

By the way, these eight strategies are summarized on the Drilling Cheat Sheet. In your first twenty Plan Bs, you may want to have it in front of you for easy reference (see figure 6.1).

To download the Drilling Cheat Sheet, go to www.livesinthebalance.org/LostandFound.

DRILLING CHEAT SHEET

Collaborative & Proactive Solutions
THIS IS HOW PROBLEMS GET SOLVED

The goal of the Empathy Step is to gather information from the child about his/her concern or perspective on the unsolved problem you're discussing (preferably proactively). For many adults, this is the most difficult part of Plan B, as they often find that they are unsure of what to ask next. So here's a brief summary of different strategies for "drilling" for information:

REFLECTIVE LISTENING AND CLARIFYING STATEMENTS
Reflective listening basically involves **mirroring what a child has said** and then encouraging him/her to provide additional information by saying one of the following:

- *"How so?"*
- *"I don't quite understand"*
- *"I'm confused"*
- *"Can you say more about that?"*
- *"What do you mean?"*

Reflective listening is your "default" drilling strategy...if you aren't sure of which strategy to use or what to say next, use this strategy.

ASKING ABOUT THE WHO, WHAT, WHERE/WHEN OF THE UNSOLVED PROBLEM
EXAMPLES:

- *"Who was making fun of your clothes?"*
- *"What's getting the way of completing the science project?"*
- *"Where is Eddie bossing you around?"*

ASKING ABOUT WHY THE PROBLEM OCCURS UNDER SOME CONDITIONS AND NOT OTHERS
EXAMPLE: *"You seem to be doing really well in your work group in math...but not so well in your work group in social studies...what's getting in the way in social studies?"*

ASKING THE CHILD WHAT S/HE'S THINKING IN THE MIDST OF THE UNSOLVED PROBLEM
Notice, this is different than asking the child what s/he is feeling, which doesn't usually provide much information about the child's concern or perspective on an unsolved problem.
EXAMPLE: *"What were you thinking when Mrs. Thompson told the class to get to work on the science quiz?"*

BREAKING THE PROBLEM DOWN INTO ITS COMPONENT PARTS
EXAMPLE: *"So writing the answers to the questions on the science quiz is hard for you...but you're not sure why. Let's think about the different parts of answering questions on the science quiz. First, you have to understand what the question is asking. Is that part hard for you? Next, you need to think of the answer to the question. Is that part hard? Next, you have to remember the answer long enough to write it down. Are you having trouble with that part? Then you have to actually do the writing. Any trouble with that part?"*

DISCREPANT OBSERVATION
This involves making an observation that differs from what the child is describing about a particular situation, and it's the riskiest (in terms of causing the child to stop talking) of all the drilling strategies.
EXAMPLE: *"I know you're saying that you haven't been having any difficulty with Chad on the playground lately, but I recall a few times last week when you guys were having a big disagreement about the rules in the box-ball game. What do you think was going on with that?"*

TABLING (AND ASKING FOR MORE CONCERNS)
This is where you're "shelving" some concerns the child has already expressed so as to permit consideration of other concerns.
EXAMPLE: *"So if Timmy wasn't sitting too close to you, and Robbie wasn't making noises, and the floor wasn't dirty, and the buttons in your pants weren't bothering you...is there anything else that would make it difficult for you to participate in Morning Meeting?"*

SUMMARIZING (AND ASKING FOR MORE CONCERNS)
This is where you're summarizing concerns you've already heard about and then asking if there are any other concerns that haven't yet been discussed. This is the recommended strategy to use before moving on to the Define Adult Concerns step.
EXAMPLE: *"Let me make sure I understand all of this correctly. It's hard for you to do your social studies worksheet for homework because writing down the answers is still hard for you...and because sometimes you don't understand the question...and because Mrs. Langley hasn't yet covered the material on the worksheet. Is there anything else that's hard for you about completing the social studies worksheet for homework?"*

Prepared with the assistance of Dr. Christopher Watson

REV 102020

LIVES IN THE BALANCE

livesinthebalance.org

Figure 6.1 Drilling Cheat Sheet

Here's an example of what drilling might sound like, with examples of some of the different drilling strategies, with a younger student:

TEACHER: *I've noticed that you've been having difficulty keeping your hands to yourself standing in line on the way to lunch. What's up?*

KAYLA: *It's not fair.*

TEACHER, USING REFLECTIVE LISTENING: *It's not fair. I'm sorry, I don't quite understand what you mean. What's not fair?*

KAYLA: *It's not fair how you do the lines.*

TEACHER, USING REFLECTIVE LISTENING AGAIN: *It's not fair how I do the lines. I'm still a little confused. Can you help me understand what you mean?*

KAYLA: *You always make me walk with you in the back of the line.*

TEACHER, ASKING A W QUESTION: *Well, yes, I've been having you walk with me in the back of the line for the past week or so because you've been having trouble keeping your hands to yourself. But now I'm trying to understand what's making it hard for you to keep your hands to yourself. Can you help me understand that better?*

KAYLA: *(shrugs)*

TEACHER, REPEATING THE W QUESTION: *Well, think about it for a minute. We're not in a rush. What's making it hard for you to keep your hands to yourself when you're in line on the way to lunch?*

KAYLA: *I want to be in front of Emily.*

TEACHER, USING REFLECTIVE LISTENING *You want to be in front of Emily. Help me understand that.*

KAYLA: *Emily's always in front of me because of the way you do the lines.*

TEACHER, USING A W QUESTION: *What is it about having Emily in front of you that you don't like?*

KAYLA: *I never get to be first in line.*

TEACHER, USING REFLECTIVE LISTENING: *You never get to be first in line. What do you mean?*

KAYLA: *I've never been first in line.*

TEACHER: *You haven't?*

KAYLA: *Never.*

TEACHER: *Because we go in alphabetical order, and you're right after Emily. You haven't had your turn at being first in line?*

KAYLA: *You skipped me.*

TEACHER: *I did?*

KAYLA: *You had Emily be first in line twice. Then we went to the back of the line again. I got skipped.*

TEACHER: *Kayla, I didn't know that. How come you didn't say anything?*

KAYLA: *I tried. You told me to be quiet.*

TEACHER: *I'm sorry, Kayla. I don't remember you trying to tell me that, but it's definitely something I would have wanted to know. I'm glad you told me now.*

KAYLA: *(nods)*

TEACHER, SUMMARIZING: *So one of the reasons you're having difficulty keeping your hands to yourself when you're standing in line for lunch is that you want to be in front of Emily because she got to be first in line and you didn't. Are there any other reasons?*

KAYLA: *Kenny keeps stepping on the back of my shoe.*

TEACHER, USING REFLECTIVE LISTENING: *Kenny keeps stepping on the back of your shoe. Is he behind you in line?*

KAYLA: *Uh-huh. He thinks it's funny when my shoe comes off. So I try to keep him from being too close to me.*

TEACHER: *And how do you do that?*

KAYLA: *I push him.*

TEACHER, SUMMARIZING AGAIN: *Goodness, I'm learning a lot here. So one of the reasons you have trouble keeping your hands to yourself is that Kenny is stepping on the back of your shoe. And another reason is that you want to be first in line because we skipped your turn.*

KAYLA: *(nodding)*

TEACHER: *Any other reasons?*

KAYLA: *That's it.*

TEACHER: *You sure?*

KAYLA: *Uh-huh.*

OK, so you didn't see every drilling strategy there, but you saw a lot of them. Don't worry, examples of Plan B with older, less congenial students are coming up soon. And we'll be taking a close look at what the next two steps of Plan B on this problem would look like soon, too. In the meantime, let's think about what was accomplished in that Empathy step. First, the teacher obtained new information that differed from her original theory. (Kayla comes from a tough neighborhood where shoving people is the norm.) She also learned why her stopgap solution (having Kayla stand in the back of the line with her) won't solve the problem durably: the solution doesn't address Kayla's concerns. Because she's solving this problem collaboratively—in partnership with Kayla—the teacher has increased the likelihood that Kayla will partner with her in solving other problems. And maybe, just maybe, the solution to this problem will be applicable to other circumstances in which Kayla is having similar problems keeping her hands to herself when she's standing in line. Nice work.

By the way, that was a quick Empathy step. Although the "average" Empathy step might last ten to twelve minutes, some early Empathy steps—with kids who have many concerns but haven't been provided the opportunity to express them—may last up to thirty minutes. But no matter how fast or slow the Empathy step, you're saving time. Because solved problems always take a lot less time than unsolved problems.

Possibility 2: The Student Says Nothing or "I Don't Know"

This is another common way in which a student might respond to your initial introduction to an unsolved problem. There are lots of reasons a kid might say nothing or "I don't know."

Your wording is off. If you don't word unsolved problems according to the guidelines in chapter 4, you'll increase the likelihood of silence or *"I don't know,"* often because the kid doesn't completely understand what you're inquiring about or believes that they're in trouble or that you're mad. Perhaps you've only been talking with them about problems when you *are* mad or they *are* in trouble, so you'll want to reassure them that you're actually just trying to understand their concerns and solve the problem together.

Your timing is off. Remember, Emergency Plan B adds heat and time pressure to the mix. Doing Plan B proactively so that the student isn't surprised by your desire to have a discussion—and giving them some advance notice of the topic—can reduce the likelihood of *"I don't know"* and silence as well.

The kid really doesn't know what their concern is about the problem you're trying to discuss. Perhaps you've never inquired about their concerns before, at least not in this way. Perhaps they've never given the matter any thought. Perhaps they've become so accustomed to having their concerns dismissed that they haven't given thought to their concerns for a very long time.

They've had a lot of Plan A in their life, and they're still betting on the Plan A horse. You'll have to prove to them—by solving problems collaboratively rather than unilaterally—that you're not riding that horse anymore. By the way, mere reassurance about that won't get the job done . . . the proof's in the pudding.

They may be reluctant to say what's on their mind. Perhaps history has taught them that if they say what they think, you'll simply disagree or take offense, and it'll cause conflict. Your goal in the Empathy step is to suspend your emotional response to what the student is saying, knowing that if you react emotionally to what you're hearing, the kid will clam up, and you won't end up hearing anything. You badly want to understand the kid's concerns, even if those concerns involve you. If you don't know what their concerns are, those concerns won't get addressed, and the problem will remain unsolved. And the kid will remain convinced that you're not listening.

They're buying time. Many kids say *"I don't know"* instead of *"Umm"* or *"Give me a second"* or *"Let me think about that a minute."* Because you're not in a rush, you'll be able to give them a second and let them think about it a minute. Many kids say nothing because they're collecting their thoughts or because they're having difficulty putting their thoughts into words. Unfortunately, adults often respond to silence by filling the void with their own concerns, theories, or solutions. In such instances, you've strayed quite far from the main goals of the Empathy step (information gathering and understanding) and made it even more difficult for the student to think. You may need to grow more comfortable with the silence that can occur as a kid is giving thought to their concerns.

If you've given a student the chance to think and it's clear that they really have no idea what their concerns are or are simply unable to put their thoughts into words, your best option is to do some *educated guessing* or *hypothesis testing*. Here, finally, your theories may actually come in handy. Suggest a few possibilities, based on experience, and see if any ring true:

TEACHER: *I've noticed that you've had some difficulty going to recess lately. What's up?*

STUDENT: *I don't know.*

TEACHER: *Well, let's think about it. There's no rush.*

STUDENT, AFTER FIFTEEN SECONDS: *I really don't know.*

TEACHER: *Take your time.*

STUDENT, AFTER ANOTHER FIVE SECONDS: *I really don't know.*

TEACHER: *Hmmm. Well, I know some things you've told me before when you didn't want to go to recess. Do you remember what those things were?*

STUDENT: *No.*

TEACHER: *Well, sometimes you're worried that the other kids will get mad at you if you mess up in the game. Is that it?*

STUDENT: *Kind of. There's some sports I'm not that good at.*

TEACHER: *Which ones?*

STUDENT: *Um . . . like basketball. And four square. But I'm pretty good in kickball.*

TEACHER: *What's hard about the other kids getting mad at you?*

STUDENT: *They take it too seriously. Takes the fun out of it.*

TEACHER: *So you said that was kind of the problem. Is there something I'm not understanding about that?*

STUDENT: *No, that's it.*

TEACHER: *Something else you've said is that when there's no organized game going on, you sometimes have trouble finding someone to play with. Is that still true?*

STUDENT: *Not so much. I've been hanging out with Omar and Katie.*

TEACHER: *So it's mainly that you're worried about the kids getting mad at you if you make a mistake?*

STUDENT: *I guess.*

TEACHER: *Well, let's keep thinking . . . maybe there's something else.*

STUDENT: *Um, when kids are being mean to each other, you're not out there, and the recess monitors don't pay attention.*

TEACHER: *No, I'm not out there during recess. Tell me more about the recess monitors.*

STUDENT: *They don't care if kids are mean to each other, even if I tell them.*

TEACHER: *What do they do if you tell them?*

STUDENT: *They just say stuff like, "Work it out."*

TEACHER: *And that doesn't help.*

STUDENT: *No.*

TEACHER: *And are you one of the kids who other kids are mean to a lot?*

STUDENT: *Kind of. But there's other kids, too.*

TEACHER: *And what are the kids who are being mean doing that's mean?*

STUDENT: *Um . . . calling names . . . and ruining people's games . . . and sometimes stealing the ball . . . stuff like that.*

TEACHER: *Well, I'm very glad you're telling me these things.*

STUDENT: *But I don't want the kids who are being mean knowing that I'm the one who told you.*

TEACHER: *No, this is just between you and me. But I do think I'm going to need some more details. Can we talk about it again tomorrow? I really want to make sure these problems get solved, now that I know about them.*

STUDENT: *What can you do?*

TEACHER: *I'm not sure, but I'd like to see if we can solve them so you can start having fun at recess again.*

Another very nice haul of information, though there are still some concerns that require further clarification. But the student's concerns are now one step closer to getting addressed . . . and the problem is now one step closer to getting solved.

As you're in the midst of hypothesizing, bear in mind that you're proposing *possibilities* rather than divining the kid's concern. Here's what divining sounds like (this is an example of what *not* to do):

TEACHER: *I've noticed that you haven't been too enthusiastic about going to recess lately. What's up?*

KID: *I don't know.*

TEACHER: *I think it's because the weather's getting colder, and you don't like going outside when it's cold. I think you're just going to have to dress warmer.*

Possibility 3: The Student Says, "I Don't Have a Problem with That" or "I Don't Care"

Many adults think that if a kid says, *"I don't have a problem with that"* or *"I don't care,"* the game is over. After all, how can they talk with the kid about a problem if the kid doesn't have a problem with the problem? But these responses aren't dead ends at all; indeed, they're the jumping-off point for learning more about the kid's concern, perspective, or point of view. Although it's entirely possible that the kid isn't as concerned about the problem as you are, that doesn't mean you can't proceed with Plan B. The first drilling strategy (reflective listening) should serve you well as an initial response. Here's what it would sound like with an older, more reluctant participant:

TEACHER: *I've noticed it's been difficult for you to get to school lately. What's up?*

DYLAN: *I don't have a problem with that.*

TEACHER: *Ah, you don't have a problem with that. I'm sorry, I'm not sure I understand what you mean.*

DYLAN: *I mean I don't really care if I come to school.*

TEACHER: *Ah, you don't really care if you come to school. Can you say more about that?*

DYLAN: *It doesn't really matter.*

TEACHER: *It doesn't really matter.*

DYLAN: *I'm dropping out as soon as I can anyway.*

TEACHER: *You're dropping out as soon as you can.*

DYLAN: *So there's not much point in being here.*

TEACHER: *Tell me more about dropping out.*

DYLAN: *There's no point.*

TEACHER: *There's no point in staying in school or there's no point in talking about it?*

DYLAN: *Um, both, I guess.*

TEACHER: *OK. Well, we don't have to talk about it, but I sure would like to know what's causing you to want to drop out as soon as you can.*

DYLAN: *I hate it here. I mean, no offense.*

TEACHER: *No offense taken. I really want to understand.*

DYLAN: *Well, you're not talking me out of it.*

TEACHER: *I wasn't going to try.*

DYLAN: *I've never done good in school. Never. I stopped trying a long time ago.*

TEACHER: *When did you stop trying?*

DYLAN: *Like, third grade.*

TEACHER: *That was a long time ago. What caused you to stop trying in the third grade?*

DYLAN: *Do we have to talk about this?*

DYLAN: *No, we don't have to. But I would like to understand.*

STUDENT: *I was getting in trouble a lot . . . and getting suspended a lot . . . and my mom was whupping me every time I got suspended . . . and I couldn't read . . . and they tried helping me with the reading, but it didn't help.*

DYLAN: *So is reading still hard for you?*

STUDENT: *Uh-huh. But I don't want anyone to know.*

DYLAN: *Your secret is safe with me.*

Good that the student talked. And it sounds like there are some concerns that have gone unaddressed for a long time. We'll have to learn more about them. Don't worry, we'll come back to that one later in the chapter, too.

Possibility 4: The Student Says "I Don't Want to Talk about It Right Now"

Fortunately, the kid doesn't have to talk about it right now, and it's a good idea to let them know that. Many kids start talking the instant they're given permission *not* to talk. If the student truly doesn't want to talk about it right now, it's likely they have a good reason; maybe they'll talk about *that.* A lot of kids *will* talk about *why* they don't want to talk about something, which is very informative in its own right. Then, after they're through talking about that, they're comfortable enough to start talking about what they didn't want to talk about in the first place.

Teacher: *Emily, I've noticed that you had difficulty working with Catherine as your math partner. What's up?*

Emily: *I don't want to talk about it right now.*

Teacher: *OK . . . well, you don't have to talk about it right now.*

Emily: *Or ever.*

Teacher: *Can you help me understand why you don't want to talk about it?*

Emily: *Because you'll tell Catherine what I say . . . or you'll make us "work it out" together . . . and I really don't feel like dealing with it. I have too much other stuff going on right now.*

Teacher: *I'd like to hear about all that you have going on right now. And I'm glad you told me why you don't want to talk about the difficulty with Catherine. I wasn't planning on telling her anything you say—it's just between me and you—and I can't make you work it out with her. So you're safe there, too.*

Emily: *It's just that she's such a know-it-all . . . and she never lets anyone else talk in class . . . and I can't stand being her math partner . . .*

Teacher: *Those are good things for me to know.*

Regrettably, many adults respond to a kid's reluctance to talk by *insisting harder* that the kid talk. But you don't want to try so hard to get the student to talk today that you lose your credibility for tomorrow. There's always tomorrow.

Possibility 5: The Student Becomes Defensive and Says Something Like "I Don't Have to Talk to You"

Let's think about why a kid would become defensive in response to adult requests for information on a particular unsolved problem. We've actually covered some of them already. Maybe they're accustomed to having adults impose solutions (Plan A), and their experience is that those solutions haven't addressed their concerns and therefore haven't worked and they don't see the point in going down that road anymore. Maybe they think that if a problem is being raised, they must be in trouble, so they're anticipating excoriation and punishment. Maybe they don't really see the point in contemplating or voicing concerns because they've become accustomed to having them dismissed or disregarded.

Fortunately, we're trying to break the patterns of communication and adult responses that would cause a kid to feel that talking is not their best option. Your best approach to defensive statements is not reciprocal defensiveness or threats of adult-imposed consequences but rather *honesty.* A good response to *"I don't have to talk to you"* would be *"You don't have to talk to me."* A good response to *"You're not my boss"* would be *"I'm not trying to boss you."* And a good response to *"You can't make me talk"* would be *"I can't make you talk."* Some reassurance that you're not using Plan A might be helpful, too, as in *"I'm not telling you what to do"* (you're not), *"You're not in trouble"* (they're not), *"I'm not mad at you"* (you're not), and *"I'm just trying to understand"* (you are). Statements such as *"I'm doing this [imposing this solution] because it's what's best for you"* would not be ideal.

You're ready to move on to the Define Adult Concerns step when you have a clear understanding of what's making it hard for the student to meet a given expectation. How do you know when you've reached that point? As you've read, keep summarizing and asking for more information (drilling strategy 8) until the student has no additional concerns.

THE DEFINE ADULT CONCERNS STEP

Presumably, you have good reasons for believing that a student should meet certain expectations. It's in this step that you articulate those reasons.

As you've read, this step is often difficult primarily because adults often rush past their concerns and start proposing (and often imposing) their *solutions.* But solutions that are proposed before identifying the concerns of both parties won't work, because they can't possibly address those respective concerns. If the student reciprocates with solutions of their own, then you and the student are now engaged in an all-too-common state of affairs called a power struggle. Power struggles result when two parties (for example, you and a student, but that's not the only possible combination of players) are proposing *competing solutions* that aren't aimed at addressing the concerns of both parties. In a power struggle, two parties are just trying to establish who has more power. In the CPS model, you're not competing on solutions. You're just trying to reach a solution that addresses the concerns of both parties. There's no such thing as *competing concerns*, either, only different concerns that need to be addressed. The concerns of one party don't trump the concerns of the other, and the goal isn't to establish whose concerns are "right" and whose are "wrong." The concerns of both parties are of exactly equal legitimacy. That doesn't mean the kid is your equal. But if you want to solve problems collaboratively with them, then their concerns are no less valid and meaningful than yours.

You'll need to give some careful thought to your concerns. Simply restating the *expectation* the student is having difficulty meeting—"*I really want to see more science homework coming in*"—would *not* be an expression of your *concerns*. Rather, your concerns will almost always fall into one or both of two categories:

1. How the unsolved problem is affecting the student (e.g., health, safety, learning)
2. How the unsolved problem is affecting others (e.g., health, safety, learning)

Expressions of adult concerns usually begin with the words "*The thing is . . .*" or "*My concern is . . .*" Let's see what some typical adult concerns might be for some of the problems we've been using as examples. At the end of each example, you'll see which of the two categories the concerns fall into.

Difficulty moving from English to social studies: *"My concern is that if you're late for social studies, you'll miss some of the lesson, and it'll be hard for you to understand what's going on."* (1)

Difficulty completing the word problems on the worksheet in math: *"My concern is that you're missing out on some important practice in math, and then the next assignment is going to be really hard for you."* (1)

Difficulty getting to school: *"My concern is that if you don't come to school, then there's no way I can help you with the things you've been struggling with . . . and that when you do come to school, you're way behind in class and sometimes distract your classmates by asking them for help . . . and that if you don't get a high school diploma, it's going to make it harder for you to get a job."* (1 and 2)

Difficulty going to recess: *"My concern is that if you don't go to recess, you'll miss out on the fun . . . and that you won't get a break from what we're doing in class."* (1)

Difficulty keeping hands to self in line for lunch: *"My concern is that someone could get hurt, and I want to make sure everyone in our class feels safe, including you."* (1 and 2).

What would the Define Adult Concerns step look like in the previous example of Kayla, the student who was having difficulty keeping her hands to herself standing in the line on the way to lunch? Maybe something like this:

TEACHER: *The thing is, I'm concerned that if you're pushing people or trying to cut in front of them, someone could get hurt. And I want to make sure that everyone in our classroom feels safe, including you. Does that make sense?*

KAYLA: *Uh-huh.*

THE INVITATION STEP

This final step involves considering potential solutions that will address the concerns of both parties, concerns that were identified and clarified in the first two steps. It's called the Invitation step because you're actually inviting the student to collaborate on solutions. The Invitation lets the student know that solving the problem is something you're doing *with* them (collaboratively) rather than *to* them (unilaterally). Notice you're not collaborating on coming up with a consequence; *consequences don't address the concerns of either party.*

To start this step, you could simply say something like *"Let's think about how we can solve this problem"* or *"Let's think about how we can work that out."* But to make things as explicit as possible, and to facilitate the consideration of solutions that will address the concerns of both parties, it's usually better to recap the concerns that were identified in the first two steps, usually starting with the words *"I wonder if there's a way . . ."* So, for one of our previous examples, that would sound something like this: *"I wonder if there's a way for us to make sure no one gets hurt in the line for lunch* [that was the teacher's concern] *and also make sure that you're first in line sometimes and that Kenny doesn't step on the back of your shoe* [those were the kid's concerns]."

Then you give the student the first opportunity to propose a solution by asking, *"Do you have any ideas?"* This is not an indication that the burden of solving the problem is placed solely on the student. The burden of solving the problem is placed on the Problem-Solving Team (the adult and student). But giving the student the first crack at thinking of a solution is a good strategy for letting them know you're actually interested in their ideas. It also gives them practice at thinking of solutions. Too often adults take on the responsibility of coming up with solutions, thereby depriving kids of the opportunity for practice. Although there is a chance that the student won't be able to think of any solutions, it's actually quite likely that they *can* think of solutions, and even ones that will take your combined concerns into account. There's also a good chance that the student has been waiting, perhaps not so patiently, for you to give them the chance.

Many adults enter Plan B with a preordained solution. In other words, they already know where the Plan B plane is landing before it takes off. If you already know where the plane is landing before it takes off, you're not using Plan B; you're using a "clever" form of Plan A. Plan B is not just a clever form of Plan A. Plan B is collaborative. Plan A is unilateral.

The reality is that there is no flight plan. The Plan B plane will head wherever the crosswinds of your combined concerns take you. But you do have some gauges in the cockpit to help you and your problem-solving partner (the student) know where to land the plane: the solution must be *realistic* (meaning that both parties can actually do what they're agreeing to do) and *mutually satisfactory* (meaning that the solution truly and logically addresses the concerns of both parties). If a solution isn't realistic and mutually satisfactory, alternative solutions should be generated and considered. By the way, the solution "try harder" is never viable.

The realistic part is crucial because Plan B isn't an exercise in wishful thinking. If you can't execute your part of a solution that's under consideration, don't agree to it just to end the conversation. Likewise, if you don't think the student can execute their part of a solution that's under consideration, then try to get them to take a moment to think about whether they can actually do what they're agreeing to do. (*"You sure you can do that? Let's make sure we come up with a solution we can both do."*)

The mutually satisfactory part is crucial, too, and requires that you and the student give conscious, deliberate thought to the concerns that the solution is intended to address. In other words, all proposed solutions are evaluated on the basis of whether they address the concerns identified in the first two steps of Plan B. The mutually satisfactory aspect is a great comfort to adults who fear that, in using Plan B, their concerns will go unaddressed and no limits will be set. *You're "setting limits" if your concerns are being addressed. And if a solution is mutually satisfactory, then by definition your concerns have been addressed.* In other words, if you thought that Plan A is the only mechanism by which adults can set limits and help students meet expectations, you were mistaken.

The mutually satisfactory part also helps the kid know that *you're as invested in ensuring that their concerns are addressed as you are in making sure that yours are addressed.* That's how you lose an enemy and gain a problem-solving partner. That's how you move from adversary to teammate, from stopgap solutions to durable ones, and from dealing with one incident after another to solving problems. Putting out brushfires was never going to work.

Early on, the student may come up with solutions that address *their* concerns but not *yours.* (And you may have a tendency to propose solutions that address your concerns and not theirs.) That doesn't mean that the student's initial solution was a bad idea—or that they don't care about your concerns or are unable to take them into account—only that they may not be skilled at coming up with solutions that are mutually satisfactory. Simply remind the student that the goal is to come up with a solution that works for both of you, perhaps by saying, *"Well, that's an idea, and I know that idea would address your concern, but I don't think it would address my concern. Let's see if we can come up with an idea that will work for both of us."*

One last important pointer. If multiple concerns are expressed in the Empathy step and the Define Adult Concerns step, there's a pretty strong likelihood that the same solution won't address them all. So before considering solutions, it's often necessary to decide which concerns will be addressed in the current discussion and which will be addressed in a later Plan B.

Many adults, in their eagerness to solve the problem, forget the Invitation step. This means that just as they are at the precipice of actually collaborating on a solution, they impose one instead.

Bummer! The kid thought you were partnering on solving a problem and then you went back to being unilateral and yanked the collaborative rug out from under them. They're likely to have major reservations about participating in the process again the next time.

Let's return to our example with Kayla to see what the Invitation step might look like:

TEACHER: *So I wonder if there's a way for us to make sure no one gets hurt in the line for lunch and also make sure that you're first in line sometimes and that Kenny doesn't step on the back of your feet. Do you have any ideas?*

KAYLA: *You could not skip me.*

TEACHER: *Kayla, I think that's a very good idea. In fact, it sounds like we owe you a time to be first in line. So we can make sure you're first in line tomorrow. Would that work for you?*

KAYLA: *Yes. How do I know you won't skip me again?*

TEACHER: *Well, this may be the first time I've ever skipped someone on being first in line. So I'm pretty good at making sure everyone gets their turns. But if I slip, please tell me again. I promise I'll be listening next time. OK?*

KAYLA: *OK.*

TEACHER: *And how about that other part . . . the part about Kenny stepping on the back of your shoes? What can we do about that so that everyone is safe?*

KAYLA: *You could always have him at the back of the line with you.*

TEACHER: *Well, there's an idea, although I don't think he'd like that idea very much. I know you didn't like that solution, so I'm betting he won't, either. And we want to come up with a solution that works for him, too. Of course, he's not part of our conversation right now, so it might be hard to come up with a solution that works for him. Do you know what I mean?*

KAYLA: *Yes.*

TEACHER: *Maybe I should talk to him about this problem tomorrow, see what his concerns are, and then maybe get together with you and him to solve the problem together. What do you think?*

KAYLA: *OK.*

Are you thinking that the three steps of Plan B with Kayla went rather seamlessly? Yes, it was pretty smooth sailing. It's good to see an initial example without major glitches. We'll be getting around to glitches in chapter 7. But let's return now to our reluctant participant, Dylan—the student who had been having difficulty getting to school—to see how that discussion turned out, too.

Continuation of the Empathy step:

TEACHER: *Your secret is safe with me. What were you getting in trouble for in the third grade?*

DYLAN: *I was, like, hyper. I couldn't sit there. And they wanted me to, like, take medicine 'cuz I was hyper. But my mom didn't want me to be on medicine. So they finally convinced her, but the medicine made me really cranky. So she didn't give it to me anymore.*

TEACHER: *And when you say you were hyper, what do you mean?*

DYLAN: *Couldn't sit still . . . had to walk around . . . couldn't do my work . . . I mean, I'm still pretty hyper.*

TEACHER: *And you'd get in trouble for that stuff?*

DYLAN: *Yup. No point in coming to school just to get in trouble.*

TEACHER: *And the work you couldn't do . . . was that just work that involved reading or other things, too?*

DYLAN: *Well, there's reading in almost everything at school. Except for, like, PE and lunch.*

DYLAN: *I suppose that's true.*

STUDENT: *Well, math doesn't always have so much reading. I was pretty good at math.*

TEACHER: *That's good to know. So school wasn't a total wash.*

DYLAN: *What's that mean?*

TEACHER: *I mean, there were some things you were good at.*

DYLAN: *I guess . . . mostly I was good at getting into trouble.*

TEACHER: *So what would happen back then when you needed to read something?*

DYLAN: *I'd ask one of my friends what it said. Then I'd get in trouble for talking. Or I'd just walk out of the class.*

TEACHER: *And they tried to help you with the reading?*

DYLAN: *Yeah, but . . . I don't know, I think I was kinda too hyper to, like, know what they were trying to help me with.*

TEACHER: *And, I guess I could look this up, but when did you stop showing up at school?*

DYLAN: *I started skipping in, like, the fourth grade.*

TEACHER: *Did your mom know?*

DYLAN: *No. I mean, she knows I don't go to school now. She gave up trying to get me to go. Now she's just worried that she's going to get into trouble if I don't go.*

DYLAN: *I suppose she could get in trouble if you don't go. Do you worry about that?*

STUDENT: *Not really. I mean, I do show up sometimes. Plus, we move a lot, so I change schools a lot, and sometimes it takes a while for them to figure out that I'm not showing up.*

DYLAN: *And what do you do when you don't show up?*

STUDENT: *Hang out. Sleep. Watch TV. Play video games.*

DYLAN: *So, this is all very good for me to know. I appreciate you telling me. Let me see if I can summarize what you've told me. It sounds like you've had trouble reading and sitting still for a very long time . . . and have received some help with the reading before, but it wasn't very helpful . . . and now you don't really see the point in showing up at school. Do I have it right?*

STUDENT: *Yep.*

DYLAN: *Is there anything else getting in the way of you showing up at school besides those things?*

DYLAN: *Well, now I stay up pretty late . . . playing video games . . . and so I don't really wake up to come to school anymore.*

TEACHER: *That's good to know, too. Anything else?*

DYLAN: *Not that I can think of.*

TEACHER: *Do you think it's still hard for you to sit in class?*

DYLAN: *Not like it used to be. Plus, a lot of times when I do show up, I'm just sleeping anyway.*

TEACHER: *Yes, I've heard that from some of your other teachers.*

Define Adult Concerns step:

TEACHER: *Well, I have some concerns about what you've told me. Can I tell you what my concerns are?*

DYLAN: *I guess.*

TEACHER: *I have a few. First, I'm really sorry reading is still so hard for you. And I'm really sorry that you didn't get the help you needed with that a long time ago.*

DYLAN: *Oh, I got help. It just didn't help.*

TEACHER: *Yes. So, that's one of my concerns. The help you got didn't help and it's still hard for you to read, and now it sounds like you've given up on reading . . . and on school in general. And my concern is that I think there might still be some ways we could help you learn things even if you're having difficulty with reading. But if you're not here, we can't help you. And if you're sleeping when you're here, we can't help you anyway. I guess my concern is that you're not going to get a high school diploma if you don't show up, and that's going to make it harder for you to get a job.*

DYLAN: *Oh, there's jobs for people like me.*

TEACHER: *Well, perhaps so. But do you understand my concerns?*

DYLAN: *Uh-huh.*

TEACHER: *So, here's the thing. I don't think we can address all of your concerns with the same solution. If it's OK with you, how about we focus on your concerns about the reading. We'll talk about the other concerns another time. That OK?*

DYLAN: *Uh-huh. But I don't think you can help me with the reading. No one ever has.*

TEACHER: *Well, maybe you're right. Maybe, in the beginning, we need a solution that doesn't focus so much on the reading. I mean, reading is what's been keeping you from learning and showing up at school. I'm wondering if we can do something about the reading so it's not getting in the way for you so much.*

DYLAN: *How would we do that?*

TEACHER: *I don't know. That's what we'd need to figure out.*

INVITATION STEP:

TEACHER: *I wonder if there's something we can do so you can learn things at school—and maybe someday get a diploma—without the reading causing you to become so discouraged that you don't even see the point in showing up. Do you have any ideas?*

DYLAN: *Well, I don't want to be in a special reading class. That's embarrassing. And it doesn't work anyway. And I don't want the whole world knowing I can't read. I wish I could learn stuff without doing the reading.*

TEACHER: *Hmmm. Interesting thought.*

DYLAN: *Really?*

TEACHER: *Yeah, really. Believe it or not, that might be possible. But if we're going to help you learn things without having to read, we'd need to do it in a way that doesn't embarrass you and doesn't let the whole world know you have trouble with reading. Yes?*

DYLAN: *Yes.*

TEACHER: *And no special reading class.*

DYLAN: *Right.*

TEACHER: *Any thoughts on how we could do that?*

DYLAN: *No.*

TEACHER: *Well, let's think about it.*

DYLAN: *Antonio gets help from that guy who comes in and tutors kids. What's his name?*

TEACHER: *I think you mean Mr. Barlow.*

DYLAN: *Yeah, old guy?*

TEACHER: *Well, I guess he's kind of old. You'd be open to having Mr. Barlow help you?*

DYLAN: *Yeah, but, like you said, not with reading. With learning.*

TEACHER: *You'd be OK with him teaching you stuff and reading some things to you?*

DYLAN: *But not in front of everybody.*

TEACHER: *He meets with kids in the conference room in the office. It's very private.*

DYLAN: *I guess we could try that.*

TEACHER: *I'll have to look into what his schedule is . . . and see if Mrs. Conant will approve it.*

DYLAN: *How come we have to talk to Mrs. Conant about it?*

TEACHER: *Because she has to approve anything we do that's not in the classroom.*

DYLAN: *She's who suspends me.*

TEACHER: *Yes, I suppose she is. I guess she's just been following the rules. But I know she very badly wants to see if there's a way for us to have you showing up and learning . . . so I'm betting she'll try hard to make this work. And we have a few other things to figure out. . . like how much time you'll be spending with Mr. Barlow—if he can do it—and how much time you'll still be in class. So I think we also have to get Mr. Perkins involved, because he would have to approve the plan, too. And he might have some other ideas for help we could give you.*

DYLAN: *I don't know him.*

TEACHER: *Well, he's not a teacher . . . he supervises all the programs of kids who need different kinds of help. But I know he'll want to make sure we have a plan that works for you.*

DYLAN: *So we have to meet again.*

TEACHER: *Yes, at least one more time. Plus, there are other parts of this problem we still need to solve. So I don't think we can come up with a complete plan today. But here's my other concern: I don't know when I can get Mr. Perkins to meet with us because I don't know his schedule. And if you're not showing up, you won't be here to meet with him.*

DYLAN: *Can't I just meet with you?*

TEACHER: *Um . . . I suppose I could talk to Mr. Perkins myself and then let you know what he says. Today is Wednesday . . . and I'm betting I won't be able to get ahold of him until tomorrow. Can you be sure to be here on Friday?*

DYLAN: *I'll try.*

TEACHER: *That would be great.*

So that problem isn't quite solved, not yet anyway. Students who aren't showing up at school often have large piles of accumulated unsolved problems, and they aren't all going to get solved in the first Plan B. On the bright side, the student did participate in the discussion, the teacher obtained a lot of information, and the student stayed engaged as they discussed potential solutions. Will he show up on Friday for the next discussion? Maybe, maybe not. Will the discussion continue the next time he does show up? Yes. All problem solving is incremental. Plan B is a process.

> "The reality is that this process will be messy, mistakes will be made, but even so, you are better off than you would have been without trying."
>
> —SCOTT, DISTRICT BEHAVIOR SPECIALIST

Q & A

Question: It's a Plan A world. How does Plan B help a kid live in The Real World?

Answer: It's not a Plan A world. Although The Real World most definitely has expectations, it doesn't impose solutions anywhere nearly as often as people think it does. More often, The Real World demands that a person identify and articulate their concerns, take the concerns of others into account, generate alternative solutions, and solve problems in a realistic and mutually satisfactory manner. Those are skills modeled, practiced, and enhanced with Plan B.

Question: All along I've been thinking that the most important role I can play in the lives of my students is to push them harder if they aren't meeting my expectations. But now I'm realizing that it doesn't make a lot of sense to simply push students to meet expectations I already know they can't reliably meet. So maybe pushing isn't my ideal role?

Answer: Not if you're interested in figuring out what's been making it hard for some of your students to meet your expectations and helping them overcome those hurdles. Having high expectations is a wonderful thing, especially if your students can meet those expectations. But if a student is having difficulty meeting an expectation, pushing won't help you identify why, won't help you partner with the student in solving the problem, and won't solve it. Your best role as a helper is problem solver, not pusher.

Question: For how long do we have to do Plan B with a kid?

Answer: Plan B isn't a temporary fix to help you eventually return to Plan A. It's a way to engage kids in solving the problems that affect their lives. Why would you stop doing Plan B?

Question: Is it OK to have a specific behavior be the focus of Plan B? Like, for example, hitting?

Answer: Remember, if you try to talk with a student about their concerning behavior, they're likely to think they're in trouble, likely to become defensive, and less likely to participate in the discussion. Also, if you talk with them about a behavior, you are, in effect, talking with them about all the unsolved problems that cause that behavior. Better to figure out what unsolved problems are setting the stage for the student to hit and try to solve those problems. Then they won't be hitting in response to them anymore.

Question: What if the kid doesn't follow through on their part of the solution?

Answer: It probably wasn't realistic and/or mutually satisfactory in the first place. Go back to Plan B to figure out why the solution didn't accomplish the mission so that it can be refined or replaced with a solution that comes closer to the mark. Remember, you don't want to sign off on a solution until you and the student have given conscious, deliberate thought to whether it's truly realistic and truly addresses the concerns of both parties. Don't get so excited that a solution has been proposed that you sign off on it instantaneously. All solutions are evaluated on the basis of whether they're realistic and mutually satisfactory. That's the litmus test.

Question: What if the solutions a kid proposes are not realistic or mutually satisfactory?

Answer: That's not an uncommon scenario for people—not just kids—who haven't had a whole lot of practice coming up with realistic and mutually satisfactory solutions. So they'll need some feedback along those lines. Such feedback might sound like this: *"Hey, there's an idea. The only problem is, I don't know if it's truly realistic for us to assume that you'll be able to make it through the entire school year without interacting with Catherine. Let's see if we can come up with a solution that you can really do."* Or *"Well, I suppose one option would be for you to just skip doing your math homework. And I guess that would address your concerns. But it wouldn't really address my concern that I really want you to get some extra practice at what we're covering in math. Let's see if we can come up with a solution that works for both of us."* In general, kids don't respond badly at all to such feedback, especially because it's being delivered in the context of a collaborative partnership.

Question: I agreed on a solution with one of my students, and it was working well for a few weeks; then it stopped working. What happened?

Answer: Although it could be that the solution you and the kid agreed on wasn't as realistic and mutually satisfactory as it originally seemed, it could also be that the original solution addressed only the concerns you heard about in the initial Plan B, but didn't (and couldn't) address concerns you *didn't* hear about. Head back to Plan B to see if you missed something. And it could also be that your initial success was due more to the quick burst of relationship enhancing that often occurs with Plan B. So it wasn't the solution working for you, it was the improved relationship. Although improved relationships are certainly a wonderful thing, realistic and mutually satisfactory solutions are even better.

Question: Should a student be punished if the solution doesn't work?

Answer: Why would you punish the student? Didn't you both agree on the solution?

Question: What if the kid says they don't care about my concern?

Answer: As you've read, you need to find out what they mean. Maybe they've had a lot of their concerns dismissed or disregarded and are now responding in kind. Maybe "I don't care" is something the kid says almost automatically in response to perceived criticism or when they feel like they're in trouble or on the spot. The long-term answer to a kid not caring about your concerns is to find out and care more about theirs.

Question: I have a classroom full of kids whose unsolved problems have been stacked up for a long time. I get that now. And I get that I need to do an ALSUP and that I need to get my priorities straight for each of them. And I get that solving those problems is going to take time. But what do I do about all the other problems while I'm working on my priorities?

Answer: Great question. Don't forget about Plan C. Early on, you may need to structure your classroom so that a meaningful number of expectations are set aside, at least for now. Doing that may not sound feasible, but your other option is even less appealing: continuing to have lots of expectations that a meaningful number of your students can't meet and that are therefore causing concerning behaviors. Remember, you inherited many of those unsolved problems. The reason the unsolved problems are stacked so high is that they haven't been solved—or even identified—previously. It's going to take a while to shake things out, and that's not going happen in one fell swoop. You're doing your students an enormous favor by structuring your classroom in a way that permits lots of problem solving and doesn't impose expectations that your students can't meet. And, eventually, a lot of those unmet expectations will start getting met.

Question: I'm having trouble imagining doing Plan B with kids younger than seven or eight years old.

Answer: Don't sell those preschoolers short! They have unsolved problems, they have concerns about those unsolved problems, and they are frequently able to participate in the process of solving the problems that affect their lives. The key variable is language-processing skills, not chronological age. I've worked with three-year-olds who were able to participate in Plan B more easily than some of the seventeen-year-olds with whom I've worked.

Question: Does CPS help kids on the autism spectrum? The ones who almost always get applied behavior analysis (ABA)?

Answer: The autism spectrum represents an extraordinarily wide range of functioning. The term *autism spectrum* tells us nothing about students' capacities to participate in the process of solving the problems that affect their lives. Again the most common obstacle is communication skills, and there are kids with communication skill delays who aren't on the autism spectrum. There are many ways (besides verbal give-and-take) to help a kid communicate about their concerns and participate in the process of contemplating and selecting solutions: pictures, sign language, assistive technology, hand signals, and so forth. If we're only relying on adult observations and solutions, we're depriving kids of the opportunity to practice solving problems, which makes them completely dependent on adults for solutions to those problems and deprives adults of information about the kids' concerns. No matter how "low functioning" a child may be, we should always be facilitating opportunities to engage them in solving problems. Dependence on adults is not a characteristic we want to promote. While there's a lot more similarity between CPS and some forms of ABA than you might think, there are also some very important differences. In CPS, adults are seeking information from the child about what's making it hard for the kid to meet expectations (some ABA practitioners rely solely on observations of behavior to divine that information). And in CPS, the child is an integral player in the process of arriving at solutions (some ABA practitioners are still assuming total responsibility for deciding on solutions and incentivizing compliance).

Question: Are there kids Plan B won't help, kids who really need to be placed in programs outside of public schools?

Answer: There will always be kids who, despite our best efforts, will need to be placed in such programs. But the reason so many kids are being placed in such programs these days—at great cost—is the large piles of unsolved problems and the extreme behaviors that are being caused by those unsolved problems. Plan B is free and, in combination with Plan C, has kept a lot of kids in their home schools.

Question: Aren't there some kids who need meds?

Answer: Yes, though nowhere near as many as are actually on meds. There are some things medication can be expected to address and things medication should not be expected to address. If we aren't aware of that differentiation, we'll see a lot of kids end up on medication for things that medication doesn't address, often because caregivers aren't sure what else to do. Now you know what else to do. Medicine is effective at reducing hyperactivity and poor impulse control, improving attention span, enhancing mood, reducing obsessive-compulsive behaviors and anxiety, reducing tics, inducing sleep, and helping volatile, aggressive kids be less reactive. There are some kids for whom medication is an indispensable aspect of treatment and who are unable to benefit from Plan B without pharmacological help. But medicine does not teach skills, and medication does not solve problems.

“What's been fantastic about CPS is it's been helping us with those kids that we couldn't figure out. You don't understand why they continue to make the same mistakes again and again—you're not sure what the concerns are. This process has been unbelievably helpful with those kids.”

—Ryan, principal

CHAPTER 7

DEBUGGING

First attempts at Plan B often don't go very well. You're new at it; the kid's new at it, too. Creating a helping relationship and using Plan B effectively take time, practice, and perseverance. So hang in there. It can take a while to feel like you have your Plan B sea legs under you. Here are some of the common problems that caregivers run into early (and sometimes later) on in collaborating with kids on solving problems.

YOU'RE NOT ACTUALLY USING PLAN B

Plan B is definitely not going to work if you're really doing Plan A. For many adults, Plan A is instinctive, a bad habit even. Some caregivers still think Plan A is going to accomplish something positive. Some adults still think the number-one goal is to teach the kid who's the boss and ensure that the kid doesn't "win." Unfortunately, throwing more Plan A at kids who haven't benefited from Plan A is an exercise in futility and frustration, for everyone.

Sometimes adults regress back to Plan A when, in the midst of doing Plan B, they feel uncertain or stuck and simply revert to something more familiar. Early Plan B discussions can be uncomfortable and messy; it's new for you and for the student. Just because you've been working with kids for a long time doesn't mean you're going to be a natural at Plan B.

Adults may also revert to Plan A in the midst of Plan B because they're a lot more focused on *their* concerns (and perhaps their solutions) than they are on the kid's concerns. Maybe it's just human nature to be more focused on your own concern than that of another person. And maybe many adults had a lot of practice having their concerns ignored or dismissed in childhood and adolescence and are simply perpetuating the cycle. But when you're using Plan B, you're as focused on clarifying and addressing the kid's concerns as you are on clarifying and addressing your own concerns.

> “There's so much that I did as a classroom teacher that I thought was good and effective in managing the behavior of my students . . . but now I think I really wasn't in touch with the needs of my students . . . I was paying more attention to *my* needs.”
>
> —Nicole, teacher educator

> Watch a school administrator make a few common Plan B errors. Go to http://livesinthebalance.org/LostandFound.

YOUR TIMING IS OFF

Plan B is, without question, a lot harder if you're trying to use it emergently. Proactive Plan B takes place under planned, less rushed, less urgent conditions, so the participants are more capable of exchanging concerns and reasoned discussion. And Proactive Plan B doesn't take place in front of the entire class, so the participants don't have the added pressure of being the center of attention, and the work of the other kids isn't being disrupted.

> "The proactive part is crucial. You never process with a person who's out of control. That's when he's the least likely to be able to process what you're saying, and you're in his face and you're saying, 'You know your choices. Either calm down or you're going to lose recess.' That never works."
>
> —SUSAN, EDUCATIONAL TECHNICIAN

It's not that the use of Emergency Plan B is a catastrophe; it's just that you don't want to make a habit of it. If you're trying to solve the same problem every day using Emergency Plan B, you're actually doing way more Plan B than is necessary. Remember, the goal is to work toward durable solutions—getting the problem solved once and for all—a task much better suited to Proactive Plan B.

But here's an example of an Emergency Plan B that went pretty well. It took place as a teacher was walking with students down the hallway to reading class and noticing that one student—it happened to be one of her students with concerning behaviors—looked quite unhappy:

TEACHER: *What's the matter, Matt?*

MATT: *I don't like my new reading partner.*

TEACHER: *You don't like your new reading partner.*

MATT: *No. Mrs. Dunleavy changed our reading partners yesterday, and I got stuck with Melanie.*

TEACHER: *Ah, I didn't know that. So you don't want Melanie as your reading partner.*

MATT: *No way! Why'd she stick me with Melanie?*

TEACHER: *I don't know . . . though I did know that you and Melanie don't get along very well.*

MATT: *Well, it's going to ruin reading.*

TEACHER: *I'm glad you told me about this, Matt. And I want to make sure we get this solved so that you don't feel that reading is going to be ruined. What do you think we can do—just for today—and then later, me and you and Mrs. Dunleavy can sit down and figure something out?*

MATT: *I don't know.*

TEACHER: *Well, think for a second. Sometimes you don't think of a solution right away, but then you come up with one.*

MATT: *How'bout I read myself today and then we talk to Mrs. Dunleavy.*

TEACHER: *So you'd read by yourself today . . . who would be Melanie's partner?*

MATT: *I don't know. She could read by herself, too. Or she could join someone else's group.*

TEACHER: *Well, let's see if either of those solutions work for Mrs. Dunleavy—just for today—and I'll see if there's a time for us to meet to talk about it before tomorrow.*

MATT: *We don't have reading group again until Friday.*

TEACHER: *Oh, right, so we have more time than I thought. You good with this plan, just for today?*

MATT: *Uh-huh.*

By the way, Plan A could make sense in some emergent circumstances, especially those involving safety when there's no viable option except to impose adult will (for example, if two kids are in the midst of a fistfight). But for many emergent safety issues, you do still have the options of Plans B and C. Plan C would make sense when you think defusing a student (by dropping the expectation that heated him up in the first place) is feasible, such as when a student suddenly balks at starting to work on a particular assignment. But, again, if we're doing a good job of identifying the lagging skills and unsolved problems of kids at risk for unsafe behavior, if we're working together to communicate and prioritize, if we're systematically solving those problems and keeping track of how things are going, if we're developing the types of helping relationships with at-risk kids that they so desperately need, then the likelihood of unsafe behavior will already have been dramatically reduced, along with the need for emergent intervention.

When I'm told that Plan B didn't work—that the kid didn't talk—I often ask the adults involved in the Plan B to tell me the story. Often the story begins with the words, *"Well, when he . . ."* This is usually a clear sign that *Emergency* Plan B was at work. I always encourage the adults to go back and do Plan B on the unsolved problem, but proactively instead of emergently. In the vast majority of circumstances, that usually does the trick.

YOU WERE IN A HURRY

It's not unusual for adults to rush through the Empathy step as quickly as possible, which contributes to an incomplete understanding of the kid's concerns. The problem, of course, is that *mushy concerns lead to mushy solutions.* If the kid's concerns are not well specified, it's unlikely that the eventual solution will solve anything.

> “One of the indicators that tells me if I am having a successful Plan B session with a student is to think about who is doing most of the talking. The goal is for me to talk very little. At my best, I am asking key questions, summarizing what the student is telling me, proposing potential solutions, and, most important, demonstrating understanding and belief in the student. When I am able to focus on my role in this process, and the student is doing most of the talking, CPS has been much more successful.”
>
> —RYAN, PRINCIPAL

Many adults find it hard to stay patient in the Empathy step. But the goal is not to get the conversation done in a nanosecond (another good reason to be using Proactive Plan B rather than Emergency Plan B). Problems that get solved in a nanosecond usually aren't durably solved. Again, you're not done with the

Empathy step until you have the clearest possible understanding of what's making it hard for a kid to meet a given expectation.

In one of the videos I show at my trainings, a wonderful elementary school teacher named Dorothy Plumpton is doing Proactive Plan B with one of her students, Bobby. The unsolved problem is that Bobby was having difficulty sitting on the floor during group lessons. The first concern Bobby articulated was that the buttons on the back of his pants might bother him. The second concern was that the floor was dirty. Fortunately, Mrs. Plumpton didn't stop there. She learned about a variety of additional concerns: that there was too much noise in the classroom, that one of Bobby's classmates was whispering in his ear, that he was frequently blamed for things he didn't do. She also learned that he was fine sitting on the floor in writing group, that he was fine reading to himself in reading group, but that he didn't like reading out loud in reading group because other kids teased classmates who made mistakes in reading out loud during reading group. If Mrs. Plumpton had stopped drilling after the first two concerns, she would have tried addressing the buttons on Bobby's pants and the dirt on the floor, but would never have known about Bobby's other concerns, in which case the problem would have remained unsolved.

> See educators Aliscia Krecisz, Dorothy Plumpton, Dave DiGiacomo, and Kate Thurman discuss their experiences with the CPS model. Go to http://livesinthebalance.org/LostandFound.

TMI

That last example brings to the fore another problem that can arise in the Empathy step: the kid talked *a lot,* and you obtained what felt like an overwhelming amount of information. Although this is a good problem to have—kind of like having too many good players on your basketball team and wondering which ones to put in the game—it does raise an important logistical issue: deciding which concerns to address in the current Plan B discussion. If we use Bobby and Mrs. Plumpton as our example, it's quite clear that one solution couldn't possibly address all of Bobby's concerns (that is, whatever solution might address the dirt on the floor wouldn't address kids giving each other a hard time if they made a mistake when reading out loud). So, as you've read, before moving on to the next two steps, Bobby and Mrs. Plumpton would have to decide which concerns to address in the current Plan B and which to save for subsequent Plan B discussions. Helping kids decide which concern to address in the current Plan B is usually accomplished by asking *Which of your concerns is getting in the way the most?* or *Which of your concerns do you think is most important?*

By the way, you'll know whether you've done a good job of identifying and clarifying concerns when you arrive at the Invitation step and try to restate the concerns of both parties. If you have trouble restating those concerns, there's a decent chance you're still lacking important information. What should you do then? Go back to the first two steps and see if there's more information to be had. Your other option is to plunge forward with mushy concerns, and you know what kind of solutions you're going to end up with if you do that.

THE KID LIED ABOUT HIS CONCERNS

It's highly unlikely that the kid lied; it's more likely that the adults thought the kid was lying. Although it's not uncommon for adults to conclude that a kid's concerns aren't "accurate" or that he's lying, we're usually wrong about that. Lying most often occurs when you're asking a kid about his *behavior* and he thinks he's in trouble. But, with Plan B, you're not asking about his behavior and he's not in trouble. Although some students fabricate because of embarrassment over their true concerns—a fairly rare occurrence, in my experience—there's really very little for a student to lie about in the Empathy step, because all you're looking for is information about what's making it hard for him to meet an expectation.

Often adults conclude that a kid is lying about his concerns when those concerns differ from their preconceived notions. Just because the kid's concerns didn't coincide with what *you* thought his concerns would be doesn't mean he's lying. Along these lines, there are basically two mistakes you can make:

1. Assuming the kid's concerns are accurate when there's a chance they're not
2. Assuming the kid's concerns are not accurate when there's a chance the kid has hit the nail on the head

The first mistake is far preferable. The price of the second mistake is much higher. Accusing a kid of fabricating—or expressing skepticism about the accuracy or authenticity of his concerns—can be fatal to the information-gathering process of the Empathy step. In other words, it causes kids—like the rest of us—to clam up or become defensive. Good drilling should eventually help you get past any potential inaccuracies and clarify the kid's concerns anyway.

The worst-case scenario is that you and the kid agree to a solution that addresses the kid's stated concern but not what turns out to be the primary or central concern, and the original solution doesn't resolve the problem. This isn't a catastrophe, nor is it grounds for pivoting to Plan A, but it is a very good reason to return to Plan B. When you return to Plan B, you'll want to suggest that there might be more to the problem than was captured by your original discussion. Here's an example of what that might sound like with Mrs. Plumpton and Bobby:

TEACHER: *Bobby, remember when we talked about how it was hard for you to sit in reading group because there's dirt on the floor?*

BOBBY: *Uh-huh.*

TEACHER: *And remember that we decided that you'd sit in a chair instead?*

BOBBY: *Uh-huh.*

TEACHER: *Well, I've noticed that it's still been hard for you to be in reading group. So I'm beginning to wonder if there are other reasons you're having difficulty sitting in reading group. Can we think about that a little?*

THE STUDENT COULDN'T THINK OF ANY SOLUTIONS

It's not uncommon for kids to have difficulty thinking of realistic and mutually satisfactory solutions in the Invitation step. Of course, many adults have difficulty coming up with realistic and mutually satisfactory solutions, too. Fortunately, even though you're giving the kid the first crack at the solution, coming up with a solution is a team effort. If he doesn't have any ideas, maybe you do. Remember, any proposals you make in the solution department are just that: *proposals.* If you're *imposing* solutions, you're using Plan A.

THE FIRST SOLUTION DIDN'T GET THE JOB DONE

Why wouldn't the first solution get the job done? As you've read, one possibility is that the solution wasn't as realistic as you and the kid thought it was. That's not a Plan B failure, just a solution that wasn't as realistic as it seemed. Go back to Plan B to come up with a more realistic solution. Another possibility is that the solution wasn't as mutually satisfactory as it seemed. That's not a Plan B failure, either, just a solution that wasn't as mutually satisfactory as it seemed. Go back to Plan B to figure out why and refine the original solution or come up with one that better addresses the concerns of both parties. It's also possible that you identified as many concerns as possible in the first attempt at Plan B on a given unsolved problem and came up with a solution that addressed those concerns. But—as in the previous example with Mrs. Plumpton and Bobby—there are concerns the solution didn't address: the ones you didn't identify. That's not a Plan B failure, just a scenario in which there were more concerns to be addressed than was initially thought. Go back to Plan B to see if there are other concerns that the original solution didn't address.

At the end of Plan B—after you and the kid have signed off on a solution and given conscious, deliberate thought to whether the solution is realistic and mutually satisfactory—it's good to acknowledge that the problem may require additional discussion. Good solutions—durable ones—are often refined versions of the solutions that came before them.

DO-OVERS

Let's take what we've covered so far in this chapter and provide an example of all the impediments that can cause things to go off the rails . . . and how to get things back on track. In this scenario, an assistant principal is facilitating a Plan B discussion with a middle school student (Jason) and his science teacher (Ms. Bradbury). See if you can spot the missteps as they're happening.

ASSISTANT PRINCIPAL: *So, Jason, the reason I asked you and Ms. Bradbury to meet with me is because Ms. Bradbury would really appreciate it if you weren't disrupting her science lab anymore.*

Looks like we need to take a do-over right from the start here. The assistant principal started Plan B with a concerning behavior, and that's going to reduce the likelihood that Jason will participate in the conversation. Let's try again.

Do-Over:

ASSISTANT PRINCIPAL: *So, thanks for meeting with me. I thought it would be good for us to try solving a problem together. Jason, you're not in trouble . . . I just want to get your take on the problem we're going to be discussing, because we're not going to be able to solve it without you. We good?*

JASON: *Uh-huh.*

ASSISTANT PRINCIPAL: *But we also need Ms. Bradbury, because we need her take on things as well. So here's the problem I thought we could work on together, at least as I understand it: difficulty completing the lab reports in science. Ms. Bradbury, can you expand on that a little?*

MS. BRADBURY: *Well, it's all the clowning around that we just can't have happening. That's why I have to separate him from his lab partner, Chris, or send him to the office.*

That was going rather well, until the "clowning around" part. It sure is hard to keep the concerning behavior out of the discussion! Let's take another do-over:

Do-Over:

MS. BRADBURY: *Well, the expectation that Jason is having difficulty meeting is completing the science lab reports while he's seated next to his lab partner, Chris.*

ASSISTANT PRINCIPAL: *OK, so, Jason, what can you tell us about that?*

JASON: *I don't know. I mean, I don't know if I'm allowed to say this, but it's kind of boring.*

ASSISTANT PRINCIPAL: *I think we're looking for you to be honest. So you don't want to do the science lab reports because it's boring. That's good for us to know.*

That was a nice stab at reflective listening, but Jason didn't actually say anything about not *wanting* to do the science lab reports.

We want to make sure that our reflective listening comes as close as possible to what the student actually said. Let's try again.

Do-Over:

ASSISTANT PRINCIPAL: *I think we're looking for you to be honest. So you're having difficulty completing the science lab reports because they're boring. That's good for us to know. Ms. Bradbury, why don't you tell us about your concerns about Jason having difficulty completing the science lab reports.*

Sorry to slow things down here, but we're not ready to move on to the Define Adult Concerns step just yet. We still need clarification on Jason's first concern, and we also need to find out if there are others. So there's more drilling to be done. Let's take a do-over.

Do-Over:

ASSISTANT PRINCIPAL: *I think we're looking for you to be honest. So you're having difficulty completing the science lab reports because they're boring. That's good for us to know. But I don't think I quite understand what you mean. What's boring about them?*

JASON: *I don't know. It's just not fun. I mean, doing the experiments is pretty fun. But writing them up isn't fun. And I'm not that good at writing anyway.*

ASSISTANT PRINCIPAL: *You sure this isn't just because you'd rather socialize than do the lab reports?*

Uh-oh. An adult theory—and one related, of course, to motivation—has just been tossed into the mix. If we stick with drilling for information, we'll likely find that this theory—like most—is incorrect. Let's try again.

Do-Over:

JASON: *I don't know. It's just not fun. I mean, doing the experiments is fun. But writing them up isn't fun. And I'm not that good at writing anyway.*

ASSISTANT PRINCIPAL: *Maybe we can find someone to do the writing for you?*

Wait, we're not talking about solutions yet, right? Best to just stick with the drilling strategies . . .

Do-Over:

JASON: *I don't know. It's just not fun. I mean, doing the experiments is pretty fun. But writing them up isn't fun. And I'm not that good at writing anyway.*

ASSISTANT PRINCIPAL: *Ah, so you're not that good at writing. Tell us more about that.*

JASON: *I'm just better at doing the experiments than I am at doing the writing. There's this whole format we're supposed to follow, and I usually get it wrong.*

ASSISTANT PRINCIPAL: *OK, so the writing part is hard because there's a format you have to follow and you usually get it wrong. Is there anything about the actual writing that's hard? Or is it mostly the format? Or both?*

JASON: *Um . . . well, I'm not very good at writing. But I think—*

MS. BRADBURY: *I think it's the format you don't like. A lot of kids don't like the format, but it's really important for you to get used to it.*

Jason was doing just fine answering for himself. We should let him continue doing that.

Do-Over:

JASON: *Um . . . well, I'm not very good at writing. But I think it's mostly the formatting part. It just makes it really confusing for me.*

ASSISTANT PRINCIPAL: *Good to know. So the formatting makes it confusing for you, and that makes it hard for you to complete the science lab reports. Is that separate from the boring part, or is the formatting what makes it boring?*

JASON: *Uh . . . well, writing the lab report is more boring than the experiment, but I think the formatting part is what makes it especially boring.*

ASSISTANT PRINCIPAL: *Got it. That's helpful. So let me summarize what we know so far . . . writing the lab report with Chris is more boring than doing the experiment, and the main thing that makes it boring is the formatting part. Yes?*

MS. BRADBURY: *And we also have the problem of you guys teasing Alicia . . . we haven't even talked about that yet.*

Well, now, moving on to a different unsolved problem really doesn't make sense here. Although it's not uncommon to stumble across new unsolved problems in the midst of the Empathy step—and although it can make sense, at times, to switch from the original unsolved problem to one of the new ones—there doesn't seem to be any reason to move off of the original unsolved problem in this instance. Let's give it another go.

Do-Over:

MS. BRADBURY: *This is good for me to know.*

ASSISTANT PRINCIPAL: *Is there anything else making it hard for you to complete the science lab reports?*

JASON: *Well, Chris is, like, making jokes the whole time. He cracks me up. So then I get in trouble for laughing.*

ASSISTANT PRINCIPAL: *OK, so Chris cracks jokes the whole time. And then you get in trouble for laughing.*

JASON: *Yeah. Well, also, sometimes I just can't stop laughing. I keep thinking about what he said, and I just keep laughing. So that's when I get into trouble.*

MS. BRADBURY: *Yeah, I don't really mind people laughing in my class, as long as it's not disrupting the work of other students. And I don't like people fooling around when we're working with the chemicals. But that's exactly right: Jason is still laughing long after everyone else has stopped.*

JASON: *It's really hard for me to stop. I wish I could.*

ASSISTANT PRINCIPAL: *OK, so now we have two reasons that it's hard for you to complete the science lab reports with Chris. The formatting of the reports makes it hard for you to write them, and Chris says things that crack you up and it's hard for you to stop laughing. Yes?*

JASON: *Yes.*

ASSISTANT PRINCIPAL: *Anything else making it hard for you to complete the science lab reports?*

JASON: *Um . . . I can't think of anything.*

ASSISTANT PRINCIPAL: *Well, give it some more thought. No rush.*

JASON: *I don't think there's anything else.*

ASSISTANT PRINCIPAL: *Well, then, let's move on to Ms. Bradbury's concerns. Ms. Bradbury, what are your concerns about Jason having difficulty completing science lab reports?*

MS. BRADBURY: *Well, it's really important that the science lab reports get done. That's what Jason is supposed to be doing after he completes the experiment.*

That wasn't really a concern. That was simply a restatement of the expectation. Remember, adult concerns fall into one or both of two categories: (1) how the unsolved problem is affecting the student and/or (2) how the unsolved problem is affecting others. Let's try that again:

Do-Over:

MS. BRADBURY: *Well, when Jason isn't doing his lab reports, he's usually talking to other kids and getting into trouble.*

Not quite there yet. Those are the concerning *behaviors* Jason is exhibiting when he's having difficulty completing the lab reports, but we still don't know the teacher's *concerns*. Let's try again.

Do-Over:

MS. BRADBURY: *Well, Jason, if you don't complete your lab reports, I won't know if you've grasped what you did in the experiment. And sometimes, when you're not doing the lab report, you're making it difficult for those around you to do theirs. Does that make sense?*

JASON: *Uh-huh.*

ASSISTANT PRINCIPAL: *OK, now we have both sets of concerns identified. So, um, Jason, I'm thinking that the best way to solve this problem is to have you partner with someone besides Chris.*

Aw, snap! Just as the threesome was about to collaborate on a solution, the assistant principal jumped back over the fence and went unilateral! Plus, that solution isn't going to address Jason's first concern, the one related to the formatting making it hard for him to do the writing. Time for a do-over.

Do-Over:

ASSISTANT PRINCIPAL: *OK, now we have both sets of concerns identified. I don't think the same solution is going to address both sets of concerns. So I'm thinking we may need two solutions: one for the formatting problem and one for the part about Chris making you laugh. Which one should we try solving first?*

JASON: *Um . . . I don't know.*

ASSISTANT PRINCIPAL: *Which do you think is getting in your way the most: the formatting concern or the concern about Chris making you laugh?*

JASON: *Probably the formatting.*

ASSISTANT PRINCIPAL: *OK, so, how are you going to meet Ms. Bradbury's expectations for writing the lab report? I know you can do it if you put your mind to it!*

Remember, the Invitation step should be a recap of the concerns of both parties, and that Invitation was simply a recap of the expectation. Recapping the concerns of both parties is really important because doing so provides a reference point for considering solutions. Plus, you want to stay away from cheerleading; enthusiasm is a wonderful thing, but it's not of much use in the solving of problems. Let's try again.

Do-Over:

ASSISTANT PRINCIPAL: *How can we make writing lab reports better for you?*

Despite the good intentions, that wasn't really much closer to the mark. Remember, recapping the concerns of both parties begins with the words, "*I wonder if there's a way . . .*"

Do-Over:

ASSISTANT PRINCIPAL: *I wonder if there's a way for us to help you with the formatting part of the science lab reports . . . and also make sure that you can show Ms. Bradbury that you've grasped what you did in the experiment. Do you have any ideas?*

JASON: *No.*

ASSISTANT PRINCIPAL: *Take your time. There's no rush.*

JASON: *Um, could I team up with someone who's better at writing them than me? Then maybe I could learn how to do it.*

MS. BRADBURY: *Well, I do want it to be your own work. But I suppose we could do that as a starting point. Marie is very good at writing lab reports. Do you want to have her help you a little?*

JASON: *I guess.*

ASSISTANT PRINCIPAL: *OK, so let's run with that solution. Thanks, guys.*

Whoa, not so fast. The litmus test for good solutions is that they be both realistic and mutually satisfactory. So we need to give conscious, deliberate thought to whether those two criteria have been satisfied. Many seemingly brilliant solutions have crashed and burned because they didn't meet the two criteria. Let's take a do-over.

Do-Over:

ASSISTANT PRINCIPAL: *Let's think about that solution. Jason, do you think that's a good way for you to get help with the formatting?*

JASON: *Yeah.*

ASSISTANT PRINCIPAL: *Ms. Bradbury, does that solution work for you?*

MS. BRADBURY: *Sure, at least in the beginning.*

ASSISTANT PRINCIPAL: *Jason, are you OK with working with Marie?*

JASON: *Not exactly. We don't really get along too well.*

ASSISTANT PRINCIPAL: *Ah, good to know. Maybe we should think of someone else?*

MS. BRADBURY: *How do you get along with Samantha?*

JASON: *Better than with Marie.*

MS. BRADBURY: *Do you want to try partnering with her instead?*

JASON: *Yeah.*

MS. BRADBURY: *But I want to make sure that Samantha isn't just doing the report for you or that you're just replicating hers. The goal is for her to teach you how to do them, yes?*

JASON: *Yes.*

MS. BRADBURY: *And Samantha sits on the other side of the room from Chris, so maybe it'll help us with that issue as well.*

ASSISTANT PRINCIPAL: *I guess we'll find out if the laughing problem gets solved with this solution, too. In the meantime, it sounds like we have a solution to the formatting problem. You're both good with it?*

MS. BRADBURY: *Yeah. I mean, I'll need to let Samantha know that I'm switching her partner and how I hope she can help Jason with the reports. But we switch partners every now and then anyway, so I don't think she'll mind.*

> “When people are learning to use Plan B, sometimes they don't do it right the first time. They may skip a step or they may slip back into Plan A. So sometimes you may not do it right, and you may slip back into your old patterns, but, eventually, with practice and with being aware and being reflective, you'll get it.”
>
> NINA, PRINCIPAL

Q & A

Question: I'm still having difficulty getting some of my students to talk in the Empathy step. Help!

Answer: Given what you've read in this and the preceding chapter, you now have a bit of a checklist for what could be getting in the way:

- *You're not really using Plan B; you're using Plan A.*
- *You're using Plan B emergently rather than proactively.*
- *Your unsolved problems aren't worded in accordance with the guidelines, so the student doesn't understand what you're asking about or is becoming defensive.*
- *The student doesn't trust you yet and is accustomed to having his concerns dismissed. Good that you're in this for the long haul.*
- *The student is convinced that he's in trouble or that you're just going to lower the boom once you get the information you're looking for. Multiple repetitions of Plan B—where his concerns are not only heard but also addressed—should help convince him otherwise.*
- *The student needs time to think about his concerns or needs help verbalizing them. Fortunately, we're not in a hurry.*
- *You're having trouble drilling for information. (Check the Drilling Cheat Sheet for help along these lines.)*

Question: But all of these impediments . . . will I ever get good at Plan B?

Answer: Well, it may seem as though there are a lot of impediments, but perhaps you're just reading about them for the first time. Think about how many impediments there were when you were learning to drive a car. The key now, as it was with driving, is practice. After you do the Empathy step for real with a student, think about how it went. If it didn't go as well as you'd hoped, reference this chapter—and maybe chapter 6 as well—and figure out why. Then try again. Little by little, you'll start to feel that you have some mastery over this process. Plan B will slow down for you. People who are new to Plan B tend to be fairly technical about it; it feels a lot more natural to people who've been doing it a while.

By the way, there's really no such thing as a Plan B failure . . . just more information that still needs to be gathered and problems that haven't yet been durably solved. So even if Plan B doesn't go as well as you'd hoped, something good happens in every Plan B. Even if you didn't identify all of the factors that might be making it difficult for a kid to meet an expectation, you still gathered some information, so you know more about the student's concerns than you did. Go back to the Empathy step the next day. Even if the solution you agreed to doesn't get the job done, at least you're partnering with a student on solutions instead of imposing your will, so the relationship- and communication-enhancing properties of Plan B are still working for you. You and the student can figure out why the original solution didn't work and come up with another one.

Question: This is not just a new way of thinking . . . it's a new way of talking, yes?

Answer: Yes. A lot of things that are said instinctively about and to students with concerning behaviors are changed when the CPS model is being implemented. Here are some examples that bring us back to an earlier chapter.

Old: *He's manipulative (or attention seeking or coercive or unmotivated or limit-testing).*

New: *He's lacking some very important skills and has problems that have gone unsolved for a very long time.*

Old: *We need to teach him who's the boss.*

New: *We need to identify his lagging skills so we're seeing him through accurate lenses.*

Old: *We need to apply consequences for his concerning behaviors.*

New: *We need to identify and solve the problems that are causing those behaviors.*

Old: *We can't let him get away with that behavior!*

New: *We are not letting him get away with anything. We're working on solving the problems that are causing that behavior. Once the behaviors subside, we'll see that he wasn't trying to get away with anything.*

Old: *He doesn't want to do well.*
New: *Doing well is always preferable . . . have we completed an ALSUP for him yet?*

Old: *He only does well when he wants to.*
New: *He does well when he can . . . when he's able to meet our expectations.*

Old: *We can't let him win.*
New: *This isn't a boxing match . . . and solving problems collaboratively is a win-win proposition.*

The things we say to students change as well:

Old: *Go to the office.*
New: *Help me understand what's hard for you.*

Old: *You have a detention, young man.*
New: *When can we get together to solve this problem?*

“ It's really important for us to consider feedback from adults who needed help from someone during childhood. The number-one thing they tell us is that somebody cared about them—somebody listened. 'Someone was there for me. And they didn't judge me and they let me talk about it and work it out.' ”

—Tom, superintendent

CHAPTER 8

THE HARDEST PART

This chapter could have been placed much earlier in the book because it describes the most challenging aspect of implementing the CPS model in a school: *organizing and sustaining the effort.* And you want to plan for this aspect before you begin trying to tackle everything else you've read about so far. But it seemed to make more sense to describe the CPS model in its entirety before getting to the hardest part. Now that you know what you're trying to accomplish, we can give more consideration to the nuts and bolts of making it happen.

Yes, it can be hard to learn to use the ALSUP, but not that hard. It just takes practice. And it can be challenging to master Plan B. But if you do it enough, self-assess how things go each time, get a handle on the routine pitfalls you seem to be falling into, guard against those pitfalls in each subsequent Plan B, and practice some more, you'll be fine. It'll start coming more naturally.

Organizing and sustaining the effort is much harder, primarily because most schools have a variety of structures in place that support the old ways of doing things. Force-fitting the CPS model into old structures isn't a great recipe for change. That being the case, a lot of those structures—related to school disciplinary policies and practices, the schedule, special education referral processes, assessment practices, the roles of administrators and school mental health staff—are likely to require modification.

GUIDING PRINCIPLES

Let's start with a few key principles to guide the effort.

1. **Start small.** It's not going to be possible to get everyone in the building good at the model in one fell swoop. Many school initiatives run aground because they're rolled out too quickly. Let's not make that mistake this time. One professional development day isn't going to do the trick, not on most initiatives and certainly not on this one. There are multiple phases to implementing the CPS model, and they're described next.
2. **Leaders gotta lead.** Transforming disciplinary practices doesn't happen without building leaders leading the way and being deeply immersed in the effort. Leaders galvanize staff. Leaders use data to help staff recognize that there's a problem that needs to be solved: we're losing many of our most vulnerable, hard-to-reach students, partially because of the ways in which we've been viewing and treating them. Leaders create time, changing schedules if need be. Leaders help staff keep their eyes on the ball, especially when the going get rough.
3. **Too many ingredients can spoil the dish.** There are many models that have been embraced by schools in an effort to transform disciplinary practices, including trauma-informed care, Positive Behavior Interventions & Supports (PBIS), and restorative practices. Although many of these models could steer a school away from punitive, exclusionary disciplinary practices, they also prescribe very different intervention practices. When schools—with the best of intentions—try to implement many

of these models simultaneously, staff members are often quite confused about what they should actually be *doing* in response to concerning behaviors and struggle to become skilled at *any* of them. So, although understandably appealing, the smorgasbord approach to transforming school discipline frequently doesn't accomplish the mission.

Each of these guiding principles is discussed in one way or another in the following sections, in which the phases of implementation are described.

PHASE ONE: THE CORE GROUP

Although a book study is a great way of introducing the CPS model to an entire staff, it's what comes after the book study that gets the ball rolling on actual *implementation.*

The usual next step is the creation of a *core group*: a cadre of staff members—usually eight to ten participants—who are going to become proficient in the model first. The core group should expect to meet weekly—usually before or after school, over a duration of approximately four to five months—to become skilled at the two key components of the CPS model: the ALSUP and Plan B. These core group members are then prepared to mentor others in the model when it comes time to expand the effort.

Who should be selected for the core group? Certainly, staff members willing to devote the time, resolve, and extra energy to practicing and mastering the key components of the CPS model. It might seem that the core group should comprise only staff members who are wildly enthusiastic about the CPS model, but it's actually good strategy to include participants who are still on the fence or even opposed, especially if they're open minded and willing to give the model a good try. Early antipathy toward the model shouldn't be viewed as a permanent state of mind; in all the schools, inpatient psychiatric units, residential facilities, and juvenile detention centers in which the CPS model has been implemented, many of those who were most resistant early on became among the most ardent advocates for the model over time.

“When we decided to implement CPS in our schools, we agreed that administrators would be trained along with counseling staff and classroom teachers. We work in a large system and staff are mandated to go to trainings and they come back and do the same thing that they had been doing before. These are good, caring people, but between severely needy students and a system that grinds out new initiatives like flour, there is no way they can separate the wheat from the chaff. By going through the training alongside my staff, I separated CPS from all of the other initiatives that they had to deal with. By letting them see me struggle with the ALSUP and Plan B, I made a clear statement that we were all going to be learners and really move in a new direction.”

—ALEX, BOROUGH PRINCIPAL

The core group should also include staff members with influence in the building; if they're excluded, there's the risk that they'll go “underground” and undermine the effort. And the core group should definitely include the principal and the assistant or vice principal. They need to get their hands dirty and their feet wet right alongside everyone else.

Perhaps the most crucial characteristics of core group members are bravery, a willingness to make and discuss mistakes, and perseverance. Changing practices and being more responsive to students with concerning behaviors can feel daunting. Becoming proficient in using the ALSUP and Plan B requires fortitude.

“The core group is where people start talking about the model and how to utilize it. It's the nucleus for everything to grow from. It can be hard, because it's volunteer and it's often after school. But it's always nice to get some of those on-the-fence people to have some successes; they have a lot of credibility when they tell their colleagues, ‘I tried this CPS thing the other day, and the problem actually got solved.’ And when they say it, their colleagues are like, ‘Oh, really. So what's up with that? How can I get some of that?’”

—TOM, SUPERINTENDENT

The core group should not spend much time debating competing views and philosophies because such debates seldom reconcile anything. Better to just get started with the key components of the CPS model. The first thing the core group should tackle is the ALSUP. Core group members should complete ALSUPs in real meetings with real staff about real students and bring those completed ALSUPs to core group meetings where members review and critique the wording of unsolved problems, with the guidelines as their reference point. Then they should do it again. And again. After three to four times, the core group members should be feeling a lot better about their skills in using the ALSUP. (Staff members who are not in the core group are nonetheless being exposed to the lenses of the CPS model by participating in meetings in which the ALSUP is being used.)

> "With the core group, you have people behind you who support you and remind you that you're doing the right thing. That's really important. Because some people are telling you you're being weak, you're not teaching the kids the right thing to do. You really need that supportive group, other people who are feeling the same way and learning along with you."
>
> —KATIE, LEARNING CENTER TEACHER

Mastery of Plan B comes next. Core group members should practice Plan B with real students on real unsolved problems, and if the school allows, audio-record the discussions and play those recordings in core group meetings. Members should provide feedback to each other on each step, with the Drilling Cheat Sheet and Plan B Cheat Sheet (figure 8.1) guiding the way. Then they should go back and do it again. And again. After eight to ten weeks, members should be starting to feel pretty good about their Plan B skills.

To download the Plan B Cheat Sheet, go to www.livesinthebalance.org/LostandFound.

DRILLING CHEAT SHEET

Collaborative & Proactive Solutions
THIS IS HOW PROBLEMS GET SOLVED

The goal of the Empathy Step is to gather information from the child about his/her concern or perspective on the unsolved problem you're discussing (preferably proactively). For many adults, this is the most difficult part of Plan B, as they often find that they are unsure of what to ask next. So here's a brief summary of different strategies for "drilling" for information:

REFLECTIVE LISTENING AND CLARIFYING STATEMENTS
Reflective listening basically involves **mirroring what a child has said** and then encouraging him/her to provide additional information by saying one of the following:

- *"How so?"*
- *"I don't quite understand"*
- *"I'm confused"*
- *"Can you say more about that?"*
- *"What do you mean?"*

Reflective listening is your "default" drilling strategy...if you aren't sure of which strategy to use or what to say next, use this strategy.

ASKING ABOUT THE WHO, WHAT, WHERE/WHEN OF THE UNSOLVED PROBLEM
EXAMPLES:

- *"Who was making fun of your clothes?"*
- *"What's getting the way of completing the science project?"*
- *"Where is Eddie bossing you around?"*

ASKING ABOUT WHY THE PROBLEM OCCURS UNDER SOME CONDITIONS AND NOT OTHERS
EXAMPLE: *"You seem to be doing really well in your work group in math...but not so well in your work group in social studies...what's getting in the way in social studies?"*

ASKING THE CHILD WHAT S/HE'S THINKING IN THE MIDST OF THE UNSOLVED PROBLEM
Notice, this is different than asking the child what s/he is feeling, which doesn't usually provide much information about the child's concern or perspective on an unsolved problem.
EXAMPLE: *"What were you thinking when Mrs. Thompson told the class to get to work on the science quiz?"*

BREAKING THE PROBLEM DOWN INTO ITS COMPONENT PARTS
EXAMPLE: *"So writing the answers to the questions on the science quiz is hard for you...but you're not sure why. Let's think about the different parts of answering questions on the science quiz. First, you have to understand what the question is asking. Is that part hard for you? Next, you need to think of the answer to the question. Is that part hard? Next, you have to remember the answer long enough to write it down. Are you having trouble with that part? Then you have to actually do the writing. Any trouble with that part?"*

DISCREPANT OBSERVATION
This involves making an observation that differs from what the child is describing about a particular situation, and it's the riskiest (in terms of causing the child to stop talking) of all the drilling strategies.
EXAMPLE: *"I know you're saying that you haven't been having any difficulty with Chad on the playground lately, but I recall a few times last week when you guys were having a big disagreement about the rules in the box-ball game. What do you think was going on with that?"*

TABLING (AND ASKING FOR MORE CONCERNS)
This is where you're "shelving" some concerns the child has already expressed so as to permit consideration of other concerns.
EXAMPLE: *"So if Timmy wasn't sitting too close to you, and Robbie wasn't making noises, and the floor wasn't dirty, and the buttons in your pants weren't bothering you...is there anything else that would make it difficult for you to participate in Morning Meeting?"*

SUMMARIZING (AND ASKING FOR MORE CONCERNS)
This is where you're summarizing concerns you've already heard about and then asking if there are any other concerns that haven't yet been discussed. This is the recommended strategy to use before moving on to the Define Adult Concerns step.
EXAMPLE: *"Let me make sure I understand all of this correctly. It's hard for you to do your social studies worksheet for homework because writing down the answers is still hard for you...and because sometimes you don't understand the question...and because Mrs. Langley hasn't yet covered the material on the worksheet. Is there anything else that's hard for you about completing the social studies worksheet for homework?"*

Prepared with the assistance of Dr. Christopher Watson

REV 102020

LIVES IN THE BALANCE

livesinthebalance.org

PLAN B CHEAT SHEET

Collaborative & Proactive Solutions
THIS IS HOW PROBLEMS GET SOLVED

① **EMPATHY STEP** | INGREDIENT/GOAL
Gather information about and achieve a clear understanding of the kid's concern or perspective on the unsolved problem you're discussing.

WORDS | Initial Inquiry (neutral observation)
"I've noticed that...(insert unsolved problem)... what's up?"

DRILLING FOR INFORMATION
Usually involves reflective listening and clarifying questions, gathering information related to the who, what, where, and when of the unsolved problem, and asking the kids what they're thinking in the midst of the unsolved problems and why the problem occurs under some conditions and not others.

MORE HELP
If the kid doesn't talk or says "I don't know", try to figure out why:

- Maybe the unsolved problem wasn't free of challenging behavior, wasn't specific, wasn't free of adult theories, or was "clumped" (instead of split)
- Maybe you're using Emergency Plan B (instead of Proactive Plan B)
- Maybe you're using Plan A
- Maybe he really doesn't know
- Maybe he needs the problem broken down into its component parts
- Maybe he needs time to think

WHAT YOU'RE THINKING
"What don't I yet understand about the kid's concern or perspective? What doesn't make sense to me yet? What do I need to ask to understand it better?"

DON'T

- Skip the Empathy step
- Assume you already know what the kid's concern is and treat the Empathy step as if it is a formality
- Rush through the Empathy step
- Leave the empathy step before you completely understand the kid's concern or perception
- Talk about solutions yet

② **DEFINE ADULT CONCERNS STEP** | INGREDIENT/GOAL
Enter the concern of the second party (often the adult) into consideration.

WORDS | Initial Inquiry (neutral observation)
"The thing is (insert adult concern)..." or "My concern is (insert adult concern)..."

MORE HELP
Most adult concerns fall into one of two categories:

- How the problem is affecting the kid
- How the problem is affecting others

WHAT YOU'RE THINKING
"Have I been clear about my concern? Does the child understand what I have said?"

DON'T

- Start talking about solutions yet
- Sermonize, judge, lecture, use sarcasm

③ **INVITATION STEP** | INGREDIENT/GOAL
Generate solutions that are realistic (meaning both parties can do what they are agreeing to) and mutually satisfactory (meaning the solution truly addresses the concerns of both parties)

WORDS | Initial Inquiry (neutral observation)
Restate the concerns that were identified in the first two steps, usually beginning with "I wonder if there is a way..."

MORE HELP

- Stick as closely to the concerns that were identified in the first two steps
- While it's a good idea to give the kid the first opportunity to propose a solution, generating solutions is a team effort
- It's a good idea to consider the odds of a given solution actually working...if you think the odds are below 60-70 percent, consider what it is that's making you skeptical and talk about it
- This step always ends with agreement to return to Plan B if the first solution doesn't stand the test of time

WHAT YOU'RE THINKING
"Have I summarized both concerns accurately? Have we truly considered whether both parties can do what they've agreed to? Does the solution truly address the concerns of both parties? What's my estimate of the odds of this solution working?"

DON'T

- Rush through this step either
- Enter this step with preordained solutions
- Sign off on solutions that both parties can't actually perform
- Sign off on solutions that don't truly address the concerns of both parties

LIVES IN THE BALANCE

REV 102020

livesinthebalance.org

Figure 8.1 Drilling Cheat Sheet and Plan B Cheat Sheet

PHASE TWO: DEMONSTRATING

After gaining proficiency with the ALSUP and Plan B, core group members are ready to begin mentoring others. Because core group members have practiced using the ALSUP in meetings, others in the building are already familiar with it (and with the new language related to lagging skills and unsolved problems). By the way, that's one of the things school staff members often notice first about the CPS model: it changes the language. Rather than talking about a student's concerning behaviors (or any variety of environmental factors that may previously have been invoked as causal factors), staff members begin talking almost exclusively about a student's lagging skills and unsolved problems. Of course, those new lenses lead to curiosity about what comes next.

The best way to get the mentoring process going is to have staff members who were not in the core group sit in as observers on Plan Bs being done by core group members. Although some people find role-playing Plan B to be useful, I often find role plays to be a bit contrived; when it comes to demonstrating, there's nothing like the real thing. It's often thought that students will be uncomfortable with another adult observing the Plan B, but I don't typically find that to be the case, though it's good to be sensitive to the possibility. This phase of the roll-out should last three to four months. The goal is to ensure that everyone in the building observes a few Plan Bs.

PHASE THREE: COACHING

In the next phase of the roll-out, Plan B novices should take the lead on a few Plan Bs, with a core group member sitting in to provide guidance, coaching, and feedback as needed. There are guidelines for such coaching and feedback later in this chapter. Over time, in the exact same way that core group members eventually became more confident and independent in their use of Plan B, the novices become more confident and independent as well. Then they aren't novices anymore. This phase should take three to six months.

Slowly but surely, staff members start to experience success with the model. They have jaw-dropping moments in the Empathy step, moments when they discover that what they *thought* was making it hard for a student to meet an expectation is *not* what was making it hard for the student to meet the expectation. They notice that kids are willing to listen to adult concerns and even take them into account in generating solutions. They have more jaw-dropping moments in the Invitation step as they discover that kids can, with some help, generate solutions that are realistic and mutually satisfactory. Problems that have been causing concerning behavior for a very long time start getting solved.

Although the timelines noted for each phase are estimates—each school has its own timing on accomplishing the mission—the schools that have had the greatest success with the CPS model didn't just "taste" the model as though they were sampling wines—they committed to *doing* it. Many found it helpful to establish specific goals, along with benchmarks and time lines for achieving those goals.

Here are some additional thoughts on teaching, demonstrating, and coaching colleagues about Plan B.

Teaching Colleagues about the Three Plans and Plan B

Let's begin with some important points of emphasis in introducing people to and teaching people about the three Plans and Plan B.

1. **Plan C is not about giving in or giving up.** The key word to encapsulate Plan C is *prioritizing.* Point out that prioritizing is important because it helps caregivers avoid trying to solve every unsolved problem in one fell swoop. Also emphasize that Plan C involves *setting aside* unsolved problems temporarily rather than dropping them forever.
2. **Both Plan A and Plan B are *attempts to solve a problem.*** What distinguishes the two Plans is that Plan A is *unilateral* and involves the imposition of a solution and (often) adult-imposed consequences and Plan B is *collaborative* and involves a partnership

between student and adult. Also emphasize that solutions that are arrived at through use of Plan A are *uninformed,* whereas solutions that are arrived at through Plan B are *informed* by the information gathered from the student in the Empathy step. Although Plan A has traditionally been emblematic of adult authority, you're much more of an authority figure when you're using Plan B.

3. **The Empathy step is where information is gathered from the child.** Without information about what's making it hard for the kid to meet a given expectation, it will be impossible to solve the problem. It's not your job to know what's getting in the way for the kid, it's your job to know how to find out. That's where those eight drilling strategies and the Drilling Cheat Sheet come in handy.
4. **Adult concerns fall into two categories.** How the unsolved problem is affecting the kid (health, safety, learning) and/or how the unsolved problem is affecting others (health, safety, learning). There's no discussion of solutions until the Invitation step.
5. **Solutions must meet two criteria.** They must be *realistic* (meaning both parties can do what they're agreeing to do) and *mutually satisfactory* (meaning the solution must address the concerns of both parties).
6. **Pre-ordained solutions are out.** If you enter Plan B thinking you already know what the solution is going to be, then you're not using Plan B. You can't even begin thinking about solutions until the concerns of both parties are identified.
7. **Plans B and C are best used *proactively*.** Thankfully, the ALSUP and Problem-Solving Plan should keep people out of the heat of the moment.
8. **Pop-up solutions are out.** A pop-up solution is a solution that kicks in when a problem has popped up yet again (for example, going to a quiet space when a problem arises). Those aren't the kind of solutions you're looking for because they don't solve problems durably . . . they just kick in when a problem

has "popped up" yet again. But problems don't actually pop up; thanks to the ALSUP and Plan B, they're predictable. So you're looking for solutions that solve the problem durably so it doesn't "pop up" yet again.

9. **The definition of a power struggle.** A power struggle is a win-lose proposition. In a power struggle, two parties are simply trying to determine who's going to win and who's going to lose. In a power struggle, two parties are simply jockeying around trying to figure out who has the power. People are most susceptible to power struggles when they skip past or ignore one another's concerns and head straight for solutions.

> "Teaching the model to others can be the most challenging task. I think it is important to remember that 'people do well if they can' just like the kids. This is such a foreign concept for some teachers and staff that it is important to be 'assumption free' with them, just as you are with the students."
>
> —Ryan, Principal

Demonstrating Plan B

Telling people about Plan B is great, but *showing* them Plan B is indispensable. As you've read, when core group members become confident in their use of Plan B, they're ready to start demonstrating its use to novices in the building. This can occur in various formats. The core group member can do Plan B with one of her own students, with the novice—having already been introduced to the three Plans and to the three steps of Plan B—sitting in to observe. Or the core group member can do Plan B with one of the novice's students, with the novice pitching in (especially in the Define Adult Concerns and Invitation steps). To help novices get the most out of the Plan Bs they observe, it's productive for the demonstrator to actually *describe* what she is doing at each step along the way. This can feel very strange to the demonstrator; but observers appreciate the connections that are made between what they've previously been told about Plan B and what they're now seeing in action.

Here are some guidelines for what to highlight in each of the steps:

Narrate the wording of the introduction. "You may remember that the introduction begins with the words, 'I've noticed that . . .' and ends with the words 'What's up?' In between, I'll insert the unsolved problem we decided we'd be talking about with Joelle today. So here goes: *Joelle, I've noticed that it's been difficult for you to write the three paragraphs on Hermann Hesse's* Siddhartha . . . *what's up?*"

Narrate the drilling strategies. "OK, Joelle's response was that it's boring. So, as you know, the first thing the kid says doesn't usually give us a very clear sense of her concern, perspective, or point of view on the unsolved problem, so now it's time for me to start drilling for more information. And I'm going to be using the drilling strategies on the Drilling Cheat Sheet that you have in front of you. The one that makes the most sense to me right now is reflective listening, which is where I'm simply saying back to Joelle what she just said to me and clarifying further. So here goes: *So, it's boring. Can you tell me more about that?*"

Continue narrating the drilling strategies each time you use one. It's very easy to get "caught up doing Plan B" and forget to tell the observer what you're doing. But what you're doing will make more sense if you're actually telling them.

Let the observer know when you're leaving the Empathy step and moving on to the Define Adult Concerns step. "OK, so Joelle has told me that she has no other concerns to tell me about on this unsolved problem. So now I'm going to move on to the Define Adult Concerns step. This is where I'm going to tell her my concern, and that usually begins with the words, 'The thing is . . .' or 'My concern is . . .' So here we go: *Joelle, my concern is that if you don't write the three paragraphs on* Siddhartha, *I'm not going to know if you read it and understood the material.*"

Let the observer know when you're leaving the Define Adult Concerns step and moving on to the Invitation step. "OK, now I've told Joelle my concerns. So next we'll move on to the Invitation. Notice, we haven't started discussing solutions yet because we had to make sure we understood the concerns of both parties first. But now we're ready. The Invitation begins with the words, 'I wonder if there's a way . . .' And what I'm going to try to do here is recap or restate the concerns we heard about in those first two steps. Ready? *So, Joelle, I wonder if there's something we can do about the fact that you're having a very hard time understanding what information I'm looking for in the three paragraphs . . . and a very hard time understanding* Siddhartha *in the first place . . . and also make sure I can know if you've read and understood the material.* And now I'm going to give Joelle the first crack at the solution—again, not because it's her job to solve the problem, but because I want her to know that I'm very interested in her ideas. So now I say to Joelle, *Do you have any ideas?*"

Narrate the processing of solutions. "All right, Joelle has suggested that maybe I could help her understand *Siddhartha* and clarify what I'm looking for in the three paragraphs after school one day. Now we need to figure out if that meets our two criteria for good solutions: they need to be realistic and mutually satisfactory. Let's do mutually satisfactory first. That's where we consider whether the solution would address the concerns of both parties. Let's think about those concerns again. I think it would address Joelle's concern that she needs help understanding *Siddhartha* and my expectations for the three paragraphs. *Joelle, do you agree?* And it would address my concern that I want to know that Joelle's reading and understanding the book. But I'm wondering about the realistic part. *Joelle, are you sure you're able to stay after school? I know you take the school bus and that makes staying after hard for you.*"

Agree to return to Plan B if the first solution doesn't get the job done. "So, it sounds like we're ready to run with the solution. I'm now going to remind Joelle that if the first solution doesn't work, we'll get together again, figure out why, and come up with a different solution."

Coaching Plan B

Let's now think more about the two most important words to characterize your efforts to coach others in the use of Plan B: *promote independence.* Your goal as a mentor is to help Plan B apprentices become increasingly independent in using Plan B, and the nature of the feedback you provide will be crucial in this regard. In other words, there's feedback and coaching that promote greater and lesser levels of independence. You don't want the apprentice to twist in the winds of Plan B, but you do want to provide feedback that promotes as much independence as the apprentice can handle.

The least independence-promoting form of coaching is to simply *take the reins* of Plan B if the apprentice is struggling (for example, *"OK, I'm going to take over here."*). Although this might be necessary in some instances—just to make sure that the Plan B goes well or to keep both parties hanging in there—it's not an especially independence-promoting approach. Somewhat more independence promoting is to *tell the apprentice exactly what to say or do* (for example, *"You need to do reflective listening here . . . say back to Joelle what she just said to you."*). This may also be necessary sometimes, especially with apprentices who are brand-new to Plan B, but it's still not going to promote much independence. Still more independence promoting is to provide more general guidance or reminders, but without explicitly telling the apprentice what to say or do (for example, *"You may want to think about whether you're really ready to leave the Empathy step just yet"* or *"Don't forget the two categories of adult concerns"* or *"You may want to think about the concerns of both parties before you sign off on that solution"* or *"I don't know if you're going to be able to address all those concerns in one Plan B."*). The most independence-promoting strategy, of course, is to say virtually nothing while the apprentice is doing Plan B (assuming it's going well). This is a sign that you've been a very good coach and that the apprentice is no longer an apprentice.

" Seeing kids who were doing poorly starting to do well is very convincing to teachers who are digging in their heels a little bit about CPS. When they see the kid starting to do well, they say, 'OK, this really does work.' And then they start trying it with the kids in their classroom.

We get that it takes time. It's not a week or a month. Literally, it is this ongoing work that in some cases, with some kids, can be years. And in the long run, it pays off. And those are the kids too that remember; they come back. They're the ones who have got you in the death grip hug when they see you again. They know on some level . . . they might not be able to verbalize it . . . what a difference it made in their lives.

I think that's why we all do what we do. I think because we love kids, we believe in kids, we want kids to do well. So when I think about that, I know there's nothing better than to be able to work with kids and make a difference. So I just feel lucky, lucky to be in a job where we get to be able to do that. "

—Kathy, teacher

PHASE FOUR: CHANGING STRUCTURES

Before we embark on this crucial, make-or-break aspect of implementation of the CPS model, it's important to restate how crucial building and school system leaders are to ensuring the success and sustainability of the change. Without question, the schools that have the greatest success in implementing the CPS model are those in which school leaders lead the way. As you read, these leaders actively participate in the process of becoming skilled in using the ALSUP and solving problems collaboratively. They help school staff recognize that transforming discipline is something the school not only *can* accomplish but *has* to accomplish; that doing well by 90 percent of the kids isn't good enough. They make sure that people stay focused on the high stakes: the fates of our most vulnerable students and what we teach all of our students about how to deal with individual differences. And they take a close look at the structures that support old ways of doing things . . . and revamp those structures so that the CPS model becomes integrated into everyday life in the building.

School Values

These days, most schools have a statement of values or mission statement. It might be a good idea to take a look at it. Does your statement of values/mission truly represent your role in the lives of your students? What are your values when it comes to individual differences? Do your practices truly align with your statement of values/mission? Does your statement of values/mission need to be changed? Do your practices need to change? Although you're differentiating instruction, personalizing learning, and universally designing, are you applying the principles and practices of these philosophies to concerning behavior? These are important questions to consider for school leaders and staff members alike.

“One of the important things to remember is that meaningful change takes time. Changing your school philosophy and culture around student motivation and behavior is incredibly meaningful. Be thoughtful, proactive, and patient. To facilitate this, building 'leadership density' at your school in the model is crucial. All the contemporary research on educational change models supports the notion that when schools build systems that allow for teacher/staff leadership and greater ownership of initiatives, then the capacity for growth and sustainability of that initiative is far more optimal over time. This approach was a key component in the success we had implementing CPS at our school. ”

—Ryan, Principal

Time

Finally! We have arrived at the four-letter word that plagues all new initiatives in schools, this one included. You've doubtless been wondering when all of this problem solving is going to be taking place, given how little time there seems to be for anything except academics.

Schools that have embraced the CPS model have had to create new structures that allow classroom teachers the time (and encouragement) to solve problems with their students. This is not a completely unfamiliar role, because teachers have always played the role of problem solver when it comes to academics, but time for problem solving is often overtaken by other priorities. As the adult closest to these problems, the teacher is usually the person best positioned to engage in problem solving. This requires regular and frequent time built into the schedule for teachers to engage in problem solving with students without detracting from crucial instructional time. (Of course, the disruptions being caused by problems that are still unsolved are detracting from crucial instructional time already.)

Finding the time to solve problems with students often begins with searching for "buried" time during the school day: before and after school, during lunch and recess, and during the teacher's prep time (if the teacher has prep time). But creating time to solve problems can involve a variety of structural changes, including flexible advisories, co-teaching, teaching teams, office hours, common study times, flexible schedules, and other flexible blocks of academic time. Perhaps the most important aspect of creating time is *coverage*. Many schools have created sophisticated algorithms to build coverage into the schedule, with administrators, school psychologists, school counselors, school social workers, and other teachers covering classrooms to allow a teacher time to do Plan B with a student. Some schools have replaced discipline referrals with problem-solving referrals, which is the means by which a teacher formally requests coverage (rather than the means by which a student is sent to the office for punitive discipline).

> “We have to value teachers' time, value what they do in the classroom, and allow them to understand that this is value added for them. When we were doing Plan B with a child, we would free up two or three other teachers to observe so they could see that we made mistakes as we went through and that it was OK to make those mistakes, and we were all learning at the same time. It's important to give people the opportunity to see it in action before they try it themselves.”
>
> —SUSAN, PRINCIPAL

My colleagues in Wisconsin, Kelly Sarah (who is a school counselor) and Rachel Policek (who is school psychologist), have also been doing something they call *pre-drilling*. They do the Empathy step with a student and are then joined by the staff member whose expectation the student is having difficulty meeting for the Define Adult Concerns step and the Invitation step. Although this is a time-saver, they appreciate that there's still tremendous added value in having the staff member be present to hear the student's concerns firsthand and in ensuring that classroom teachers and other staff members know how to do the Empathy step themselves.

In order to support this work, administrators, parents, and teachers need to embrace the idea that time spent on problem solving is not lost to academic learning but is an investment in deeper engagement. In addition, there are opportunities in group work, in projects, and in the natural course of academic learning to integrate social emotional learning and problem solving. If classrooms develop procedures and language for students to raise concerns between students in the natural course of academic work, then the learning embedded in a CPS approach is reinforced universally with all students.

> “If we don't take the time to do Plan B, then we are sabotaging ourselves because of all the time it takes to repeatedly 'discipline' the same kids. So on a selfish, adult level, if we don't take time to do this, then we're spinning our wheels, doing the same ineffective things over and over again.”
>
> —CAROL, PRINCIPAL

Although I fully appreciate the concerns about time, I find that *commitment* is the bigger issue. Once schools commit to solving problems with students, they find and make the time to do it.

Meetings and Special Education Referral Mechanisms

Although the lagging skills and unsolved problems identified on the ALSUP can inform IEPs, FBAs, and behavior plans, it is possible that the ALSUP will also make these time-consuming components obsolete, at least for some students. In other words, if the ALSUP is the standard pre-referral, triage instrument in your building, you may not need a full-blown IEP, FBA, or behavior plan. You may not need a special education referral or testing. Meetings don't have to be primarily focused on whether a student qualifies for special education; once you identify a student's lagging skills and unsolved problems, the student's need for special education services will become clear.

Reluctant Participants

One thing is pretty much guaranteed: some staff members are going to struggle with and passively or actively resist the change. Some people find the tenets of the CPS model to be at odds with their own thinking or training. It's important to clarify whether there's actually much thinking behind the thinking. There are so many clichés applied to students with concerning behaviors (see chapter 2), and those clichés so often take on lives of their own that initial reactions to the CPS model often aren't based on deep philosophical beliefs but rather on those clichés. Gently challenging clichés can be productive. Drilling strategies may help here as well.

“I can remember one particular teacher who, at times, would butt heads with students. This teacher had high expectations and truly cared about students but would often find herself in a standoff with a particular student. The teacher and I sat down with the student so I could model a Plan B session with them. Afterwards, in debriefing with the teacher, her first comment was that she could not believe ‘how much the kid talked,’ and she said, ‘I have a completely different view of him now.’ She also shared that, even after some training with the model, she still felt that she wasn't confident in what to do. This experience had really helped her learn how to apply the structure of the model in a specific and meaningful way with a student. This teacher, who could have been a ‘saboteur’ to the process at our school, became one of our big advocates of the CPS model.”

—Ryan, Principal

Ultimately, once everyone in the building has been involved in ALSUP meetings and the ALSUP has become the standard pre-referral, triage instrument in the building; once everyone in the building has been exposed to Plan B and had some practice and coaching; then the ALSUP and Plan B become the *expectation* for how students with concerning behaviors are handled. Until that happens, staff members may feel that the ALSUP and Plan B are optional. Once they are no longer optional, then it becomes crystal clear which staff members are having difficulty meeting those expectations and school leaders must find out what's getting in the way of the expectation being met. As you'd imagine, those conversations begin with the words, “*I've noticed that . . .*”

“It takes time to change people's mind-sets, depending on their existing beliefs. When some people learn about CPS, it clicks right away because their heart is aligned with it. But there are a lot of people whose mind-set isn't there, whether it's because of tradition, their own experiences, or whatever. They are in one belief system that says the reward-and-punishment model is going to be effective; you've just got to keep doing it harder and bigger to make it work. So hearing about a different model doesn't click with them. They need to see it; they need to experience it before they're going to be able to make a change. It can take a long time to change that mind-set. And in some places, just the fear of change can be pretty big. ”

—Carol, principal

Engaging Parents

At some point along the way, you'll want to involve parents in the collaborative effort as well. I've seen some schools involve parents from the get-go; others wanted some time to get comfortable with the CPS model before involving parents. Either approach is OK, but if you choose to hold off, don't wait forever.

Over the years, a lot of the parents I've worked with have stated that they felt blamed and uninformed by their children's school, that they haven't felt heard by school personnel, and that teachers and administrators were very keen on Plan A, not only in interactions with the kids but also in interactions with the parents. Amazingly enough, many teachers had some of the same complaints about the parents! What's clear is that Plan B is just as applicable to teacher-parent problem solving as it is to teacher-student problem solving.

“ We used to say things like that a kid doesn't get any support from his parents with his homework. But what do we know about that family? We know nothing. We really don't know what happens at home. The kid still needs us to do our thing at school. If we know the kid is not going to get the homework support at home, we need to solve the problem with the kid so that the work can get done at school. ”

—Alanna, teacher

Here are a few statements of the obvious. Blaming is remarkably counterproductive, even if it seems clear that a student is going home to a situation that is less than ideal. And imposing your will on others (Plan A) is not the ideal path to fruitful collaboration and communication.

“When I was a principal, I was often put in a position where I felt like I had to be a bad guy with the parents. And I can remember feeling so uncomfortable that parents thought I was angry with them or that it was their fault. But once you start partnering with them . . . now I can see them anywhere, and they're happy to see me, and when I say, 'How is your child doing?' they're so open about it. It's not an adversarial relationship.”

—VICKI, FORMER DIRECTOR OF COMMUNICATIONS

Yes, many kids who exhibit concerning behaviors at school are going home to problematic family circumstances. But many well-behaved kids come out of less-than-ideal situations, too. And many kids with concerning behaviors come out of seemingly idyllic families. Yes, many kids who exhibit concerning behaviors at school exhibit many of the same behaviors at home, but that just means that the kid is struggling to meet expectations in multiple environments, and that the problems that are causing those behaviors haven't yet been solved in those multiple environments. But that also means that the adults in those different environments have shared concerns and frustrations. And that should make collaborating easier, not harder.

“We had a year when we had a lot of pushback from parents of well-behaved kids. It was turning into a witch hunt. They wanted to see immediate consequences for misbehavior. They wanted to see that these kids were punished for what they were doing. Their own children were telling them that the behaviorally challenging kids weren't getting punished for what they were doing. But we called all the parents together, and there was a lot of anger about the kids who were acting up in school. Then I met with each parent individually. And I listened to them. A lot of what they were upset about was stuff that was in the grapevine and simply wasn't true. But when they heard what we were trying to do, and how we were trying to help the most vulnerable kids in our building, they completely chilled. We have nothing to hide in helping our tough kids. The year after that, those parents were integral to helping us create the learning center in our school, where kids and teachers go to get help solving problems together.”

—NINA, PRINCIPAL

Do the home folks need to be a party to every Plan B that takes place at school? No. In fact, the home folks don't need to be involved in *most* of the Plan Bs that take place at school, because the unsolved problems don't involve them. Some unsolved problems at school do involve the parents—for example, truancy, tardiness, incomplete homework—but most do not. So although it's a very good idea to keep parents informed of the problems being solved at school, their actual involvement in Plan B is frequently unnecessary.

“ We worked really hard to team with parents and at showing them respect and empathy. I mean, we're often aware of their home life. But there's no judgment. Parents do well if they can, too. Certainly if it was unsafe, we would do what we're mandated to do. But we've seen how parents change and become partners with us. I think teachers sometimes forget how uncomfortable coming to school is for a lot of parents . . . especially the kind of parents whose homes don't fit the standard definition of ideal. We have a lot of transient families, and if we lowered the hammer on them, they'd move away. They would just go to another school. They would disappear. ”

—KATHY, TEACHER

And what about circumstances in which efforts to collaborate with parents aren't going well? The very same pitfalls that apply to adult-child problem solving are equally applicable to adult-adult problem solving (see chapter 7). For example, using Plan A instead of Plan B. Using Emergency Plan B instead of Proactive Plan B. Failing to identify and clarify the concerns of both parties. Dueling solutions (power struggles) are a big one. If all else fails, never forget that you can still do a kid a lot of good in the six hours a day, five days a week, nine months a year that she's in school, even if her parents aren't involved in the effort. And that the kids who are going home to situations that aren't ideal need the folks at school to be on their game more than ever.

Too Many Ingredients Can Spoil the Dish

Many schools are so devoted to transforming school discipline that they try to implement many different programs that will help them achieve the goal. And there are many appealing programs that could help them move in the right direction, including—as mentioned—trauma-informed care, PBIS, and restorative practices. But there are some fundamental differences between these models and CPS. This section is in no way intended to dismiss or disparage these other models but rather to highlight important differences.

Trauma-informed and trauma-responsive care has helped many caregivers become more aware of the adverse childhood experiences that affect the lives of many kids, has helped caregivers be cognizant of the physiological basis of the fight-or-flight reactions of these kids, has enabled people to respond more empathically to these kids, and has emphasized the importance of relationship building. However, when it comes to what people should actually do with this information, frequently the answer is *do CPS.* That may be because CPS isn't about using power (power would be the last thing you'd want to use with a kid with a trauma history), gives kids voice and agency (exactly what you'd want to give kids who have been traumatized), eschews the use of hands-on procedures such as restraint and seclusion (using those procedures on kids with trauma histories can best be described as re-traumatizing the already traumatized), pinpoints the specific lagging skills and unsolved problems that may (but also may not) be attributable to the child's trauma history, and improves communication and relationships between caregivers and kids.

Admirably, PBIS has encouraged caregivers to view concerning behaviors through the same lenses as other developmental delays and has discouraged the use of punitive disciplinary strategies. However, true to its behavior-analytic roots, PBIS still focuses primarily on *behavior* (that's what the *B* in *PBIS* tells you) and still emphasizes the use of reinforcement to teach and reteach replacement *behaviors.* There's really no emphasis in PBIS on solving the problems that are causing those behaviors. And although PBIS does emphasize the teaching of skills, the skills being referred to are *behavioral* skills (for example, standing in line, sitting at one's desk, raising one's hand); there is little or no emphasis on the *cognitive* skills found on the ALSUP that help caregivers view kids with concerning behaviors through completely different lenses. Those skills, as you now know, are not trained primarily through reinforcement schedules or check-in/check-out, but through solving problems collaboratively and proactively. PBIS has not been transformative enough to change things for many kids at Tier 2 and Tier 3. Can CPS be implemented within the three tiers of PBIS? My colleagues Rachel Policek and Kelly Sarah have done just that in two school systems in Wisconsin (see www.livesinthebalance.org/research, 2021).

Though the research on restorative practices has been underwhelming, it has nonetheless helped many educators move from punitive disciplinary to practices that are instead focused on restoring relationships and repairing harm. And restorative circles do, at least in some ways, resemble the problem solving that takes place in CPS. However, there is still an emphasis in restorative practices on concerning *behaviors*; it is those behaviors that students are making amends for. But making amends doesn't solve the problems that are causing those behaviors, and if those problems are being solved, there's nothing for students to make amends for.

Trying to combine these models—or implement them simultaneously—with CPS can be too much of a good thing, very confusing, and, in some important ways, incongruent. Transforming school discipline is hard enough; implementing multiple models simultaneously doesn't make it easier.

Q & A

Question: I'm still a little concerned about the time issue.

Answer: One of the reasons it's so important to have building leaders integrally involved in the implementation process is that they're often in a position to create time, whether by providing coverage or rearranging schedules. But, as you read, the key factor here is *commitment* to making the time. If time is left to random chance, there won't be much Plan B going on nor many problems being solved.

Many schools have implemented something called 15 Minutes a Day. This involves every teacher in the building committing to carving out fifteen minutes every day to solving problems with individual kids. That's seventy-five minutes a week. Five hours a month. Forty-five hours every school year that every teacher in the building is committing to solving problems with kids. Best to start with the kids with concerning behaviors, the ones causing the most disruption to their own learning and that of others. If you're systematic and diligent about it, you're going to get a lot of problems solved with those kids over the course of the first three to four months. Then it's time to turn to the others.

By the way, the others have probably noticed what you're doing. I had an elementary school teacher tell me that after three to four months of doing 15 Minutes a Day, one of her well-behaved students approached her and asked if he could have one of those slots, as he had something he wanted to talk with her about. She was both surprised and eager to hear the unsolved problem he needed help with.

“In our building, we were able to create a space that we turned into the problem-solving center. We call it the learning center. And we placed in the room one of our gifted education techs who has been using the model for about two or three years and has a wonderful way with children. That's her space, and she works with all the children. So any teacher who feels that a child needs to access that space can meet with the learning center teacher to do an ALSUP and create a plan, and the children can do problem solving with the teacher of the learning center or with a classroom teacher. And it's a very soothing environment. Some kids and teachers access the learning center a lot; others less so. But it's a place where they have lots of Plan B going on. It's been very successful. At first, some people thought that the learning center is where kids who act up go to play. So people were thinking, 'Well, they're being reinforced for their negative behavior, because they're choosing to act out to be able to go and play.' And that was not the case at all. It was a misperception. ”

—Nina, principal

Question: Who should do Plan B with a given student on a particular problem?

Answer: Early on, it will presumably be a member of the core group, because core group members are the only staff members dedicating time and practice to becoming proficient in the model. But, as you've read, once that happens, core group members start inviting other staff members to sit in on and observe Plan Bs so that they have a feel for the process. Then those staff members start trying to lead Plan B discussions with a core group member sitting in to provide coaching and feedback. Then, just as the core group members did, those staff members start trying Plan B independently.

Eventually, *the ideal person to do Plan B with a student is the staff member whose expectation the student is having difficulty meeting.* What if the relationship between that student and staff member is so far gone that Plan B feels impossible? Have someone else—someone the student is most likely to talk to—lead the Plan B, perhaps with the staff member sitting in as well. If things go as hoped, eventually the staff member and student will be able to do Plan B together without facilitation by someone else.

Question: There are a lot of initiatives for students with concerning behaviors these days, more than the ones already mentioned. Can you speak to those as well?

Answer: There is significant congruence between the goals, structure, and practices of Response to Intervention (RTI) and the CPS model. For the unfamiliar, the impetus for RTI comes, at least partially, from the recognition that the needs of many students receiving services in special education could be met in general education classrooms. Thus the first and most important school personnel to implement intervention are classroom teachers. The CPS model is an excellent fit with RTI in this regard. RTI also represents an attempt to introduce scientific, data-based methods into school classrooms to guide the selection, use, and evaluation of academic and behavioral interventions. CPS is a good fit along these lines as well.

There is also substantial overlap philosophically between CPS and Marshall Rosenberg's Nonviolent Communication (NVC) model, with some nuanced differences. The NVC paradigm places a heavy emphasis on empathy, clarifying concerns and feelings, and ways in which people communicate with one another that interfere with empathy and compassion. Although the precepts of NVC and CPS are congruent, CPS places a significantly stronger emphasis on lagging cognitive skills as the crucial factor contributing to challenging behavior.

Thomas Gordon's Teacher Effectiveness Training model shares many important themes with CPS as well, again without the emphasis on lagging cognitive skills and unsolved problems.

There are also crisis management models that overlap to some degree with the CPS model. But CPS isn't best thought of as a crisis management program. Crisis management programs are aptly named, because they're oriented toward *managing* crises. Although it's good to know how to defuse and de-escalate a crisis—and Emergency Plan B is useful along these lines—CPS places significantly greater emphasis on crisis *prevention.*

Question: Is CPS truly realistic in a middle, junior, or senior high school, where kids have multiple teachers who don't always have a chance to communicate with one another?

Answer: Many middle and high schools are organized in teams or learning communities, which makes collaboration and communication easier. Nothing takes the place of ensuring that staff members have the time to talk about high-priority kids and meet periodically (preferably, at least weekly) to monitor the kids' progress and modify the Problem-Solving Plan. Again, the only models of care that don't require good communication are the ineffective ones.

Question: I'm a school principal. I've been trying to help my teachers use CPS, and it's gone pretty well. But I have a few teachers who just aren't doing it. Advice?

Answer: Try to figure out why, starting with the Empathy step, as in *"I've noticed that you haven't been participating much in our CPS work. What's up?"* They may not be convinced about the rationale for Plan B. They may feel they don't have the skills to do Plan B yet. They may feel completely overwhelmed. They may be retiring soon and just don't see the point. They may have a bad case of initiative fatigue. We won't really know what their concerns are unless we ask. Then we can work toward ensuring that their concerns—and yours—are addressed. If CPS becomes the expectation for how teachers will handle unmet expectations in their classrooms, then we want to make sure those teachers get as much support as they need.

Question: Earlier you mentioned that the ALSUP could inform the IEP? Can you be more specific?

Answer: If you've identified a kid's lagging skills and unsolved problems (through use of the ALSUP) and established a set of priorities (through use of the Problem-Solving Plan), you're ready to incorporate those priorities into an IEP. You're also ready to document how Plan B will be used to address those lagging skills and problems. You can find an example of an IEP that incorporates the language of CPS at www.livesinthebalance.org/LostandFound. And you'll find an example of a 504 Plan that incorporates the language of CPS in the same place.

Question: I'd like to incorporate CPS into my FBAs and Behavior Intervention Plans . . . are there examples of those as well?

Answer: Sure thing. You can find examples at www.livesinthebalance.org/LostandFound.

Question: How can we tell if our school is making progress in our handling of behaviorally challenging kids?

Answer: There's no single benchmark signifying that you've arrived, given that improvement is an ongoing process. But there are some pretty clear indicators:

- The mentality toward who are struggling kids in your school is oriented toward lagging skills and unsolved problems, and people are routinely using the ALSUP in their assessment of these kids and the Problem-Solving Plan in monitoring their progress.
- Staff members are skilled in and actively using Plan B.
- Structures supporting the use of CPS are in place, including mechanisms for (1) responding to problems proactively rather than emergently; (2) communicating and collaborating across staff members and with parents; (3) practicing, coaching, and monitoring Plan B skills; and (4) orienting new staff members to the model.
- Mechanisms are in place for the continuous evaluation of school discipline, and discipline referrals, detentions, suspensions, and expulsions are dramatically declining. Many schools that have implemented the CPS model have completely eliminated discipline referrals, detentions, and suspensions.

“Plan B has really made a huge impact on our students, but it also affected our thought processes, the language we used, and the way we interacted with students. It was pretty life changing for all of us. I've been in other buildings, and I've seen teachers demand that a principal send a kid home for misbehaving. And then the principal is on the phone with the parents telling them they have to come pick up their kid. And it's like, oh my gosh, why? What will that accomplish?”

—KATHY, TEACHER

CHAPTER 9

FRINGE BENEFITS

Most of what you've been reading in the prior eight chapters has been specific to kids with concerning behaviors. But, of course, they're not the only students in your building or classroom. What about the rest of 'em? Is the goal to have two different discipline programs in the building, one for the kids with concerning behaviors and one for everyone else? Why would you want to deprive the well-behaved kids of the good stuff? Don't they have problems that need to be solved as well?

No, it's not the goal to have two different discipline programs in the building. As you know, you don't need your traditional discipline program for the well-behaved kids, because the traditional discipline program isn't why they're behaving themselves in the first place. Yes, you want to be using Plan B with well-behaved kids, too, because no matter how well behaved they are, at some point they'll have difficulty meeting certain expectations and may need your help getting over the hurdle. If, as recommended in chapter 8, you get Plan B rolling with the students with concerning behaviors, you'll find that you start to have more time to solve problems with everyone. Everyone gets the help they need.

"Kids now understand when another kid is having a hard time, and that it's OK. So if a child needs to leave the room or go for a walk, I used to think the other kids would say, 'That's not fair. I want to go for a walk, too.' But that's not what they say. They say, 'Oh, he's just having a hard time. He'll be back later. He's getting what he needs.'"

—KATIE, LEARNING CENTER TEACHER

But helping students surmount the factors that are making it hard for them to meet certain expectations isn't the only reason you want to use Plan B with everyone; *you also want to foster skills on the more positive side of human nature*—skills that help kids treat each other kindly and with mutual respect, like empathy, appreciating how one's behavior is affecting others, taking another's perspective, honesty, and resolving disagreements in ways that do not involve conflict. It is when these skills are present that kids and other human beings display sensitivity, acceptance of individual differences, compassion, and cooperation. And it's when these skills are absent that the more malignant side of human nature—insensitivity, conflict, aggression, dismissiveness, and destruction—rears its head.

Are the ways in which we're disciplining, teaching, and interacting with our students—and solving the problems that affect their lives—fostering those skills? Regrettably, in far too many places and instances, the answer is no.

In an age in which so many schools are implementing community-building programs and emphasizing social and emotional learning, what are we doing wrong?

We're still doing way too much Plan A. And Plan A begets Plan A.

Fortunately, Plan B begets Plan B. As you read in chapter 2, teachers have historically been among the most important agents of socialization in society. When we tell teachers to prioritize high-stakes testing and achievement—to the neglect of the skills that help humans display the more positive side of human nature—we do ourselves and future generations an enormous disservice. When we use power to solve problems with our kids, we teach our kids to use power to solve problems.

The reality is that we all want our concerns to be heard and validated. And we all want our concerns to be addressed. People—kids included—become demoralized, marginalized, disenfranchised, alienated, and increasingly prone to hopelessness and sometimes violence when those two things don't happen. The collaborative resolution of problems is perhaps the most important aspect of improving a school's culture and climate.

“I think it's important to remember that the social and emotional aspect goes hand in hand with academics. I think it's hard for teachers. We have all these things that we have to teach. We have to meet standards. But students are not going to be able to meet those standards if they don't deal with the social-emotional part first.

At the beginning of each school year, I let the entire class know that I'll be talking with them about different things that might come up. It's the same language no matter which kid it is and no matter what the problem. So the kids really get used to the idea, 'Oh, I see her really being open to working with kids, and I know that it's OK if something happens in the classroom, that she's going to be there to help all of us.' The kids start to see you as a partner.”

—KATHY, TEACHER

But there are additional benefits to implementing the CPS model in a school, including enhancement of soft skills, eliminating of the use of restraint and seclusion, and reducing disproportionality.

ENHANCEMENT OF SKILLS

In some schools—especially those where staff members are cognizant of the reality that preparing kids for high-stakes tests is actually very poor preparation for the demands of The Real

World—there's been a movement toward the teaching of what are called "soft skills," including critical thinking, perseverance, the ability to collaborate, and the ability to benefit from feedback. The instruction in these schools is more project based and student centered, as opposed to the mere teaching of factual information. But we need to go further. Besides project-based and student-centered learning and community building, what additional technology is needed?

Well, you've been reading about it in this book. We know how to ensure that kids' concerns are heard, clarified, validated, and addressed and that solutions are mutually satisfactory. We know how to ensure that kids feel a sense of agency. That same technology helps us teach, practice, and display the characteristics on the more positive side of human nature.

Let's consider how that might be. The first step of Plan B—the Empathy step—helps students practice thinking about and clarifying their concerns. It also helps them articulate concerns in a way that increases the likelihood that those concerns will be taken into account and addressed. What a crucial life skill! So often, we human beings—kids included—exhibit our least desirable traits when we have a concern and can't articulate what it is. Sometimes that's because we're convinced our concerns won't be heard, because the person we're interacting with isn't giving us the chance to voice them. Sometimes it's because the emotions associated with the concerns have flooded in too quickly, so we end up expressing powerful emotions rather than the concerns driving those emotions. And sometimes we react in mere anticipation of a battle. The Empathy step slows things down for everyone, and helps ensure that we're focused on the right currency: collaboration, not power.

What do students learn in the Empathy step? They learn that their concerns are valid and will be heard and addressed rather than being dismissed, disparaged, or belittled. What do adults learn in the Empathy step? They practice and model how to listen, to empathize, and to take another person's concerns into account.

Why are teachers frequently so surprised to learn their students' real concerns? Often because they've never heard those concerns, sometimes because they've never really asked. Kids whose concerns are heard and taken into account are far more receptive to listening to and taking into account the concerns of others.

"When I was a kid, I was well behaved at school. But I remember how painful it was to watch kids get in trouble year after year as a student. You'd be like, 'Please don't . . .' You almost want to wish them back into their seat or wish . . . 'Please do your paper. You're just going to get in so much trouble.' And then to have them get yelled at in front of everyone. So it's really nice now when kids see us solving problems with them, and not just with the difficult kids but all of them. We're who we want to be now. We're modeling who we want them to be and how we want them to treat each other."

—KATIE, LEARNING CENTER TEACHER

A student's ability to communicate about their concerns is vital because concerns are the currency of Plan B and because durable, mutually satisfactory solutions must address the concerns of both parties. But that ability is important not only for participating in Plan B; it's important in life.

There are many young people in the world—I've worked with some of them in prisons and residential facilities—who have been on the receiving end of society's most punitive, exclusionary interventions for a very long time. Many of them have given up on being heard and understood. But they still recognize when someone is listening, taking their concerns seriously, and working to ensure that those concerns are addressed. That's when we start to see that they still have the capacity for the better side of human nature.

Students learn and practice many skills in the Define Adult Concerns step as well, including listening, empathy, taking into account another person's perspective, and appreciating how one's behavior is affecting others. These are, without question, among the most important skills in the human repertoire. They play a huge role in helping us treat each other with compassion and sensitivity. They help us refrain from conduct that is harmful to others. Although rules and laws and enforcement are wonderful, these are external controls, and they aren't very reliable when it comes to fostering the better side of human nature. The goal is for the controls to be *internal*, and that just doesn't happen without giving kids practice at taking into account the concerns of other people. Yet the manner in which we often go about solving problems at school doesn't teach these skills at all! If you're using Plan A, then you're teaching the exact opposite: you're not listening, nor being empathic, nor taking into account the student's perspective, nor demonstrating an appreciation of how your behavior is affecting them.

> "I have a teacher who has embraced the model to the level where she does not just use CPS with highly challenging students; she uses it with all her students and builds it into her day. It is a reminder that often universal strategies for instruction, which benefit struggling learners, can be of benefit to all students. Whenever this teacher begins with *'I've noticed that . . .'* to one particular student, he always smiles and says to her, 'It must be problem-solving time again!'"
>
> —Ryan, principal

We humans are vulnerable to being so convinced of the correctness of our position that we justify some of our worst behaviors with the belief that we're right. This is where we confuse the legitimacy of our *concerns* (which is a given) and the assumed justifiability of the *solutions* we're imposing, and lose track of our empathy and concern for others. If you're imposing solutions, it's guaranteed that someone else's concerns are being swept away. This is not what we want to be teaching students. And it's not how we want to go about solving problems with our students, either.

The Invitation step also teaches students valuable skills, including considering the likely outcomes or consequences of one's actions; considering a range of solutions to a problem; shifting from one's original plan, idea, or solution; and taking into account situational factors that would suggest the need to adjust a plan of action.

How does the Invitation do that? Let's revisit what's going on in this step. You and the student are considering solutions and evaluating the degree to which proposed solutions are realistic and mutually satisfactory. The realistic part gives you and the student invaluable practice at gauging whether both parties are capable of reliably executing their part of a solution. And the mutually satisfactory part gives you and the student practice at ensuring that the concerns of both parties are addressed.

I'm often asked if I ever come across problems that simply cannot be solved in a mutually satisfactory manner. The answer is no. But what I do come across are lots of scenarios in which people have concluded that a problem is unsolvable because their competing solutions cannot be reconciled. That's because they've leapt right over concerns and jumped straight into solutions, which couldn't possibly take into account the concerns of both parties.

As you know, there's no such thing as competing *concerns.* One party's concerns are no more compelling or more important than the other's. Both parties' concerns need to be clarified and addressed. So the only reason a problem would be unsolvable is that there's no way to address the concerns of both parties. In my experience, that is a very rare occurrence.

ENDING RESTRAINT, SECLUSION, AND CORPORAL PUNISHMENT

The focus on eliminating the use of restraint and seclusion (R & S) procedures and Corporal Punishment in schools has gained new momentum, perhaps due, in part, to the documentary film *The Kids We Lose,* produced by Lives in the Balance, but also due to legislative initiatives at all levels of government. Unfortunately, training on the use of R & S procedures is standard fare for many classroom teachers, especially those working with kids with social, emotional, and behavioral challenges. For a long time, training in such procedures was also the norm in inpatient psychiatry units, residential facilities, and prisons until many such treatment facilities made a concerted (and successful) effort to reduce their use of these procedures.

There's a common belief that R & S procedures are necessary for keeping kids and staff members safe. This point of view is completely at odds with the reality. Kids and adults frequently get hurt during restraint and seclusion incidents. Moreover, to my knowledge, there is absolutely no science supporting the belief that R & S procedures improve safety. Indeed, experience tells me that *reducing* the use of R & S *reduces* injuries to staff members and kids.

There is also the belief that R & S are necessary behavior management tools. They are not.

And there is the belief that R & S are "crisis prevention" strategies. As depicted in figure 9.1, they most assuredly are not. Nor is de-escalation. By the time the behaviors that signify that a student is becoming escalated occur, caregivers are already very *late.* The sequence of events leading to use of R & S—the sequence of restraint and seclusion—is actually quite straightforward, but it begins *way before* those behaviors occur.

In the first bubble there is a known, predictable expectation a child is having difficulty meeting. If that problem is identified

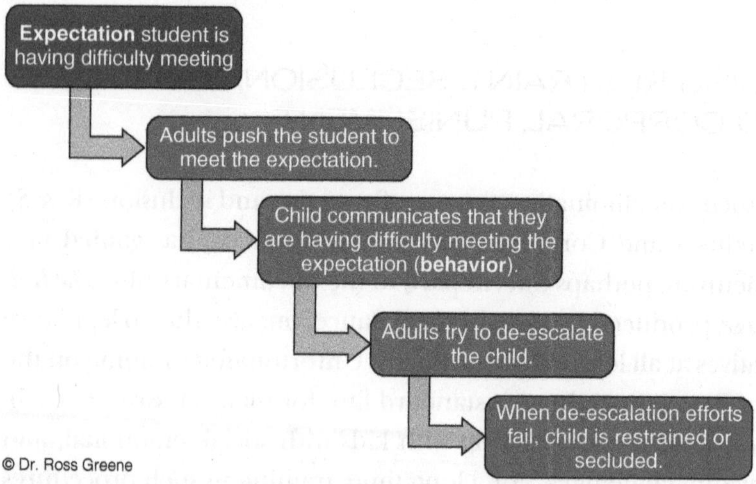

Figure 9.1 Sequence of Restraint and Seclusion

and solved—proactively—the rest of the sequence is never set in motion. That's what would happen if the CPS model were being used. In too many places, what happens instead—the second bubble—is that caregivers try to get the kid to meet the expectation anyway, often by insisting or pushing harder, in the erroneous belief that insisting and pushing harder will elicit better performance. Then—this is the third bubble—the kid exhibits behavior to signal that they are having difficulty meeting the expectation. We're now rather late in the sequence. That's right, the behavior is *late.* And interventions that are focused on behavior are focused on what's *late.* If the behavior is "unlucky," the adults will conclude that the student is becoming escalated and deploy de-escalation strategies (the fourth bubble). We are now very late. And if the de-escalation strategies don't work, the adults will deploy R & S procedures (the fifth bubble). We are now very, very late. And if we're very, very late, we couldn't possibly be in crisis *prevention* mode. Identifying and solving problems collaboratively and proactively is as early as it gets.

As you know, another key component of the CPS model involves giving very serious consideration to whether kids can actually meet the expectations being placed on them. That's early, too. If the kid can't meet the expectation, it's worth pondering why those expectations are being placed on the child in the first place. The standard answers—*"That's what the other kids are expected to do"* or *"That's what we expect from sixth graders"* or *"That's something he's going to have to do on standardized tests"*—are completely at odds with special education law and differentiation. Having a student endure countless restraints and seclusions because of expectations we already know they can't reliably meet makes no sense whatsoever.

No one wants to restrain or seclude a kid. A very long time ago—before I went to graduate school—you would have found me restraining and secluding kids in an inpatient psychiatry unit in Miami, Florida. I hated it, partially because the kids were usually bigger than me, but especially because it quickly began making no sense to me. It became clear that intervening once kids are already escalated is horrendous timing. And it became clear that many kids do not calm down when they have adults pinning them to the ground. And—perhaps most important—it became clear that R & S procedures do not solve the problems that are causing the kids to spin out of control in the first place. This experience eventually contributed to the creation of the CPS model.

Published research has shown that the CPS model is highly effective at dramatically reducing and ultimately eliminating the use of R & S in inpatient psychiatry units, residential facilities, and prisons. And see figure 9.2 for data from a school system in Maine that had relatively high rates of R & S before implementing the CPS model in the 2019–2020 school year (pre-COVID).

But schools and school staff members frequently work at a disadvantage, especially compared to child and adolescent inpatient psychiatry units, even though the populations of both settings are frequently quite similar. Medication management on inpatient units is tightly controlled and monitored; in many special

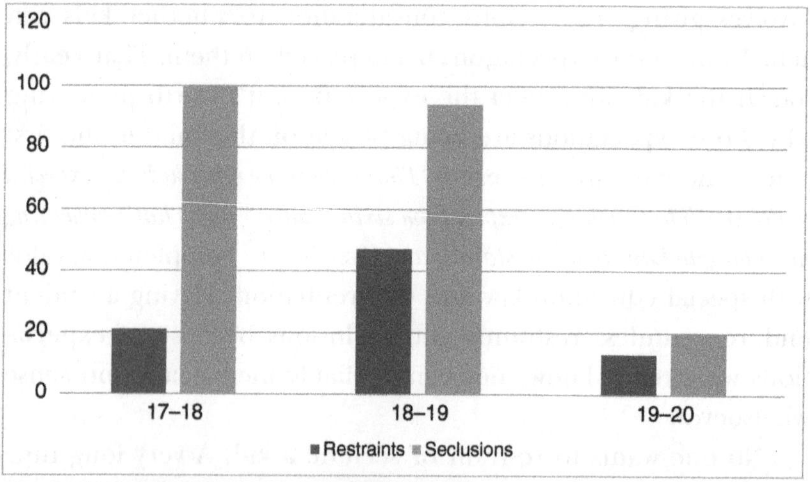

2017–2018: September 12, 2017–June 15, 2018

2018–2019: September 11, 2018–June 4, 2019

2019–2020: September 2, 2019–March 13, 2020

Figure 9.2 Restraint and Seclusion Three-Year Comparison

education classrooms, staff members are unaware of what psychotropic medications a child is taking, have little contact with prescribing physicians, and are often unaware of changes to a child's medication regimen. In schools—even in special education classrooms—there is great pressure to teach, even though many of the children in such classrooms are only sporadically available for learning. In such classrooms, there is often great reluctance to temporarily suspend expectations in the service of stabilization.

> “Whenever I hear about a kid being shackled or manhandled at school—as we've seen in the media recently—I say to myself, 'I wish that kid was at our school. I wish we had a chance with him.' Because I think we would have known that the student had a lot of lagging skills and unsolved problems and was having a hard time, whether it was behavioral or friendships. But we're solving problems with them so they have better ways to solve problems than violence. You find out what's behind it. Instead of just saying, 'You don't mean that; now I'm going to have to call your parents,' we say, 'What's going on that's making you feel that way?' And then you help them solve that problem.”
>
> —KATIE, LEARNING CENTER TEACHER

The reality is that restraint and seclusion are acts of desperation, they do not keep anyone safer, are not therapeutic, are the result of a treatment failure, and simply indicate that we're late.

As for corporal punishment, it is hard to fathom that kids are still being hit—that's right hit ... by adults ... with a piece of wood—in American public schools close to 100,000 times every year. Harder still to imagine how anyone who works with children would think that striking a child is an effective way to accomplish anything, let alone solve the problems that are affecting their lives. It's a national embarrassment.

ENDING DISPROPORTIONALITY

The release of the US Department of Education's Office for Civil Rights (OCR) 2017–18 Civil Rights Data Collection makes clear that although admirable efforts have been made to address the disproportional use of exclusionary and punitive disciplinary practices in public schools, the mission has yet to be accomplished. Black and (to a lesser degree) Hispanic students still face significantly higher rates of punitive, exclusionary methods of discipline as compared to their White counterparts.

In response, many schools have embraced antiracism, cultural competence, and/or cultural humility training, helping their educators and administrators to embrace more informed views about Black and Brown students. These programs can heighten awareness of the ways in which systemic racism may contribute to disproportionality and have actuated efforts to address them. In many schools, the focus on disproportionality has caused a reexamination of disciplinary practices in general. Indeed, although Black and Brown students are clearly overrepresented in statistics regarding the use of punitive and exclusionary discipline, such discipline is still most frequently applied to White students, for whom it is also counterproductive and unnecessary.

Researchers have been focused on the factors contributing to disproportionality for several decades. Catherine Kramarczuk Voulgarides and Natalie Zwerger—in a paper from the Steinhardt Institute at New York University—have summarized this research and encapsulated the complex factors contributing to disproportionality, including (1) discipline policies and practices; (2) the subjectivity of special education referral processes; (3) instructional practices that place Black students at a potential disadvantage; (4) unequal access to educational opportunities; (5) racial disparities in how school staff interact with parents and the quality of services and education they receive; (6) biased teacher perceptions of student capabilities based on race; (7) cultural mismatch between school staff, families, and students; and (8) the sociodemographics of a school and school system.

More specifically, the research tells us that disproportionality begins at very early ages. Studies have shown that although Black children make up only one-fifth of all preschool students, they account for over half of preschool suspensions. The chasm continues into older ages: the suspension rate for Black high school students (24.3 percent) is significantly higher than the rate for their White counterparts (7.1 percent).

We know that children who experience punitive discipline at school have lower academic achievement, suggesting that lost time at school adversely affects achievement, potentially exacerbating existing race-based achievement gaps. A single suspension in ninth grade considerably lowers the odds that a student will graduate from high school or enroll in college.

We also know that exclusionary practices do not improve students' behavior; that suspensions typically result in grade retention, academic difficulties, poor attendance and delinquency in students; and that students who are suspended or expelled have higher rates of being involved with the juvenile justice system or incarceration as adults. Students who frequently access punitive school discipline—and who fall behind academically due to missed time in school—are at risk for disengaging from school and may begin to affiliate with peers who have had similar experiences, fueling the school-to-prison pipeline.

We know that White students tend to be suspended for different behaviors (such as smoking and cutting class) than Black students (talking back to a teacher or being disrespectful). A common theme in research related to bias is the tendency to interpret the behavior of Black students as disrespectful or insubordinate.

Finally, we know that a key factor in the outcome of an office referral is the administrator's perspective on discipline and a school district's support of punitive discipline practices.

To address disproportionality, researchers have underscored the need to completely re-envision school discipline. If punitive, exclusionary disciplinary practices are being disproportionally applied to Black and Brown students, then it stands to reason that practices that are not punitive and exclusionary would be a potential remedy.

There are various facets of the CPS model that would mitigate many of the factors that are contributing the disproportionality.

First, as you know, the CPS model does not focus primarily on overt behavior; it focuses on the expectations that a student is having difficulty meeting that is causing challenging behavior. As a result, the potential for biased interpretations of behavior is reduced. Moreover, when behavior is no longer the focal point of intervention, the application of punitive behavior modification strategies no longer makes sense. As you also know, in the CPS model, the primary goal of intervention is for caregivers and kids to engage in collaborative efforts to solve those problems. For many students—especially those who have been on the receiving end of punitive discipline for a long time—the Empathy step is often the first time they've had the opportunity to talk about what they were going through and what was making it difficult for them to meet a particular expectation.

> “I think CPS has allowed us to be more compassionate. I've heard teachers from other schools talk about our school. They were saying things like, 'Oh, you let your kids do whatever they want.' And I got really defensive and said, 'That is such a misconception.' People can say what they want, and that's just noise. You have to remember that.”
>
> —Alanna, teacher

For reasons reviewed previously—but also because of expected developmental variability—some students have more unsolved problems than others. Disproportionally solving problems with students—rather than disproportionally applying punitive discipline aimed at addressing the behaviors caused by those problems—would be a very positive development.

Efforts to heighten the sensitivity of educators to racial bias and to better understand the experiences of their Black and Brown students are indispensable. Efforts to help educators become more sensitized to the traumatic experiences of many of their students and to understand how such trauma may affect behavior are equally important. However, it is crucial that educators also be provided with alternative tools to address the unsolved problems that are contributing to concerning behaviors. Research has shown that solving problems collaboratively and proactively with students is an extremely effective way of improving children's behavior, is at least the equivalent of behavior modification strategies, and has been shown to dramatically reduce or eliminate discipline referrals, detentions, suspensions, and the use of restraint and seclusion. (A paper by Greene and Winkler [2019] describing the accumulated findings of the effectiveness of the CPS model in families, schools, and therapeutic facilities can be found at www.livesinthebalance.org/research). These findings are consistent with others that have shown that interventions emphasizing empathic discipline can reduce discipline incidents among male Black students.

> "I've worked with the toughest of the tough. The kids that I worked with were not greeted with open arms by the school. And yet they keep coming to school every day. Every day they wake up and think maybe things will be different. Maybe someone will talk to me. Maybe someone will listen to me."
>
> ALEX, FORMER BOROUGH PRINCIPAL

Thus, it is possible to envision a day when schools no longer deploy discipline referrals, detentions, suspensions, paddling, restraints, and seclusions. This would require a complete transformation of the structures of discipline in many schools, a process many schools have embraced. What is required is vision, commitment, and a desire to change things for the better for all students (Greene, R.W., & Haynes, S. 2021, https://www.livesinthebalance.org/research).

Q & A

Question: Can I use Plan B to involve my entire class in solving problems that affect all of them?

Answer: Absolutely. If there are unsolved problems that affect the entire class—often related to how kids are treating each other but also related to things like hallway and cafeteria comportment—then it makes perfect sense to have the entire group voice concerns and work toward mutually satisfactory solutions. Here's a video of a full-class Plan B: https://vimeo.com/338514777/e6cda88d0e.

Question: I'm beginning to recognize that we're not merely talking about how we should be solving problems with students; we're talking about how people should be solving problems with people. And I'm starting to think that my principal and superintendent need to learn more about Plan B.

Answer: Well, now, that wasn't a question; it was a statement!

Question: I get it now. There are many things going on in my school that are not helpful and about which I can do nothing. But there are enough things about which I and my colleagues can do something that we can still make a huge difference in the lives of our most vulnerable students.

Answer: I couldn't have said it better myself.

> " The reason we're working with children is that we're passionate about them and we want to teach them. We don't only want to teach them academic skills. We want to teach them social skills, too. A very important part of being human is learning those skills, like empathy. That's why we're here. We're here to help kids. And a teacher's time is very precious. You can feel the pressure of the mandates and everything like that. But we're taking the precious time that we spend with kids working on those skills. Kids are worth the investment of our time. "
>
> —KATIE, LEARNING CENTER TEACHER

You've arrived at the end of the book, but hopefully your journey is just beginning. Don't stop here! If you are committed to improving outcomes for your most vulnerable students, the lenses and practices articulated in the foregoing chapters should help you get you there. If you are committed to improving the culture and climate in your building, what you've read should help you get there. There's a lot at stake. Our most vulnerable, at risk kids are counting on you. I can't wait to hear about all the kids you helped.

INDEX

NOTE: Page references in italics refer to figures.

B

C